Mary Tyler Moore

Mary Tyler Moore

Jason Bonderoff

ST. MARTIN'S PRESS
NEW YORK

Library of Congress Cataloging in Publication Data
Bonderoff, Jason.
    Mary Tyler Moore : a biography.
    1. Moore, Mary Tyler, 1937–   . 2. Entertainers—
United States—Biography. I. Title.
PN2287.M697B36   1986   791.45′028′0924 [B]   85-25086
ISBN 0-312-51887-0

10 9 8 7 6 5 4 3 2

Contents

Mary Tyler Moore

1

Perfect Child ... Perfect Wife ... Perfect Casting

In 1979, when Robert Redford was preparing to direct *Ordinary People*, he had no trouble imagining the perfect leading lady. To Redford, Mary Tyler Moore seemed like ideal casting as Beth Jarrett, the stylish, tennis playing, taut-as-steel mother that the script of *Ordinary People* called for. "I knew we needed someone you could 'like' in the part," he later said, "because Beth is likable on the surface. She is, you know, the all-American girl."

And who, after all, is more all-American than Mary Tyler Moore?

Who indeed? Yet appearances can be deceiving. Despite that image we have of Mary tossing her hat in the air on a Minneapolis street corner, the real Mary Tyler Moore didn't have a Midwestern Protestant upbringing at all. She's an Irish Catholic girl, born in Brooklyn, New York, the daughter of a man who worked for the electric company. Unlike Beth Jarrett or Mary Richards, WJM's immortal news producer, the real Mary isn't college-educated either. She barely finished high school. And if she ever had to find her way around Illinois or Minnesota, she might easily wind up in Japan. Mary has spent her entire life living in New York City and Los Angeles. She's only been to the Midwest on a few sparse occasions: to film the opening and closing credits of *The Mary Tyler Moore Show* in Minneapolis, and to do some location work on *Ordinary People* in Lake Forest, Illinois.

If anything, her own life starts out more like *A Tree Grows in Brooklyn,* at least as far as the early scenery is concerned. Mary Tyler Moore was born on December 29, 1937, in Flatbush—a Brooklyn neighborhood where quiet, tree-lined streets and one-family houses with small front yards predominated. Some people had Fords or Hudsons, but everybody took the elevated subway train—not cars or taxis—when they traveled to Manhattan to catch the live shows and the latest Clark Gable movie at Radio City Music Hall. Mary's family, like most, were not especially rich—nor were they especially poor.

Mary's mother, the former Marjorie Hackett, was Protestant; her father, George Tyler Moore, was Catholic. But there was no confusion about how their children were to be raised. Mary, the eldest, and later her brother John and her sister Elizabeth, were all baptized into the Roman Catholic faith. When it was time for kindergarten, Mary was enrolled in Saint Rose of Lima parochial school.

Mary was born at the tail end of the Depression, just when the country was starting to revive. America's entertainment styles reflected the new sense of optimism. Shirley Temple, tap-dancing to the tune of "The Good Ship Lollipop," was America's number one box-office star. People were humming "Alexander's Ragtime Band," reading *Gone With the Wind,* and rooting for Little Orphan Annie. It was the calm before the storm. In 1939, war erupted in Europe, and America would not remain untouched for long.

Pearl Harbor came just a few weeks before Mary's fourth birthday. But for Mary, the most memorable part of the next few years wasn't the food-rationing or the blackouts, but the big, patriotic war musicals that MGM and all the other movie studios began churning out. As a little girl, Mary loved watching musicals on screen, especially the dancers. When she was five, she saw Jimmy Cagney in *Yankee Doodle Dandy* and for days afterward she marched up and down the street, waving a flag and pretending to tap-dance across the deck of an imaginary battleship. Romantic musicals were even more enticing. Mary would dress up like Ginger Rogers and fantasize that Fred Astaire was whirling her round and round in an elegant ballroom or, better yet, whisking her off to Rio.

A few of her neighborhood playmates were taking tap and ballet lessons—Shirley Temple had made it a must along with long curls—and when Mary got wind of it, she convinced her mother to sign her up, too.

Dance class quickly became her life, an all-consuming passion that left little time for friends or other after-school activities. She was constantly practicing—and going to class just to watch even when she didn't have a lesson of her own. Once she started dancing, Mary never walked; instead she floated on her own special cloud of fantasy. By the time she was eight or nine, Mary had become a social outcast. Well-behaved, quiet, and composed—totally lost in a world of her own—Mary was the kind of "best" little girl that other girls steer clear of.

In his biography *The Real Mary Tyler Moore*, Chris Bryars hypothesizes that dancing for Mary was a way of winning her father's approval. During the day, Mary would listen to the radio, making up steps to the tunes she heard, and at night she would put on a private recital for an audience of one—her dad. It may be that such scenes actually occurred; but Mary's creative drive was also a kind of compensation for her performance in another area where she couldn't succeed—at school. Mary was never a good student—something her father couldn't understand. He, after all, was a magna cum laude graduate of Georgetown University, a man who read constantly and valued learning. By her own admission, Mary had little interest in school or books. So, if she couldn't please her father academically, then entertaining him became the only way to hold his attention.

But things changed as she grew older. She began to sense her father's defects and to feel that he had let her down, too. If her report card was less than exceptional, his climb up the professional ladder didn't rate an A either. His lack of ambition baffled and disappointed her. Yet in some ways Mary knew she was a carbon copy of her dad. Her dark English-Irish good looks came from him; so did her stand-offishness. She secretly hoped she hadn't inherited his lack of aggressiveness, too.

She once told *McCall's* magazine that her father had "absolutely no career drive. I can't account for that. He was an enigma to me. I won't say cold, but reserved. It's only in the last ten years that we've learned to express affection openly. I think that a lot of my career drive is based on a childhood need to get Daddy's approval and attention."

Even as an adult, she still carried that need with her. It influenced her choice of men. All three of her husbands have played the Protector in some way. Mary married for the first time when she was still a teenager; her husband was twenty-eight and what attracted her most was his maturity. Her second husband, producer Grant Tinker, orchestrated her rise to megastardom, built a multimillion-dollar business empire around her, and exercised almost total control of her career for most of their married life. Her current husband, Dr. Robert Levine, hardly qualifies as a father figure, but in some ways he's a safe harbor for

Mary, too. How could you feel more protected than by marrying your doctor? Especially when you're a diabetic who needs frequent medical attention?

Even in her career, Mary has often played out the father-daughter theme. Her longest-running co-star was Edward Asner, who portrayed her very paternal boss, Lou Grant, on *The Mary Tyler Moore Show.* Interestingly enough, Mary has never become particularly close with leading men her own age. But she has always found her directors—the men who controlled her on the set—far more fascinating. After making *Ordinary People,* Mary struck up an intense friendship with Robert Redford. Later she dated Michael Lindsay-Hogg, who directed her on Broadway in *Whose Life Is It, Anyway?*

She's never collected many women friends, either. For a long time, she felt she wasn't good at it, that she didn't know how to make friends or keep them. During her five years on *The Dick Van Dyke Show,* she and Rose Marie were hardly soulmates off the set; and during her *MTM* years, she didn't broaden her circle. Grant and Mary occasionally socialized with Betty White and Valerie Harper and their respective husbands, but those ties never fell into the category of tight friendships. In the late 1970s, Mary had a dance studio built onto her California house and a whole bunch of neighborhood housewives, who were ex-dancers, would come over to work out with her. They'd drink her diet soda and ask her gossipy questions about Robert Redford. But Mary never felt close enough to any of them to open up and confide that her marriage was falling apart or that her son was giving her a tough time. It was only that double loss—first the death of her son, then divorce from Grant (whom she had once called "my best friend")—that finally forced Mary to make some difficult changes in her life. Today, for the first time, she truly has women friends —a wide and stimulating variety of them—and she considers this a top priority in her life.

Years of therapy helped her see the pattern of isolation that she had started creating in childhood. "I was always kind of quiet, a loner," she admits, so in a way it wasn't hard for her to leave Brooklyn, with the rest of her family, at the age of ten. She had no strong attachments to sever. And she was excited about moving to Los Angeles. It was Uncle Harold—the family success story—who prompted the move. He was a vice president of MCA and he kept sending letters home from Beverly Hills, telling all about the sunshine, the palm trees, and his golfing dates and lunches with Bob Hope. Eventually Mary's father decided to follow Harold's lead and resettle in Southern California. For Mary, the move meant an immediate change for the better. She got to enroll in the prestigious Ward Sisters School of Dance Arts, and she was now only a bus ride away from MGM, where she was sure that someday she would star in big movie musicals and become the Ginger Rogers or Ann Miller of her generation.

Mary went to Immaculate Heart High School in Los Angeles, but she had only a passing interest in her classes or in after-school activities. "I was totally starstruck," Mary recalls. "The only thing I read in high school was show-business stuff. I couldn't keep my mind on *Return of the Native,* but I devoured every gossip column in the newspapers." She collected star memorabilia, too. Her autographed photos of Dean Martin and Jerry Lewis stayed with her till the day she married Grant Tinker. She knew what she wanted to do with her life—dance!—and it had nothing to do with catechism or trigonometry.

Religion had become a major source of conflict both at school and at home, especially when Mary turned fourteen, blossomed out, and discovered boys. When the nuns told her that prolonged kissing was a mortal sin, Mary decided that prolonged advice from the nuns was a waste of time.

She often felt her mother had no time to listen to her—and even when she did listen, she had no understanding of her point of view. Her mother was constantly busy with the younger children. Her brother, John who was eight years younger than Mary, was only in grade school when Mary was sixteen; and when Mary was already married, her mother, who had recently converted to Catholicism, gave birth to a third child, Elizabeth.

For long stretches of time, Mary moved in with her Aunt Birdie and her maternal grandmother, who gave her the sympathy and encouragement that were somehow lacking at home. By the time she was in high school, Mary was staying with them permanently, and only visiting her parents on weekends. Years later, Mary told writer Michael Ver Meulen that the decision to move out was strictly hers. "Sure, I think I was being a rotten kid," she admitted, "but there were parts of what they did in raising me that were a little rotten, too."

At the same time, she was trying—unsuccessfully—to break into movies and television. She'd finish her last class in high school and rush off to some agent's office in downtown Hollywood, waving a letter of recommendation from her Uncle Harold and launching into a long spiel about how long and how hard she had studied dancing. "Most of the agents wanted to help and were very nice," she recalls, "but they had no way of knowing if I was just a crazy kid or if I really had any talent."

Her persistence was bound to pay off, and the day after she graduated from Immaculate Heart, Mary landed her first professional job in television. She was cast as the Hotpoint Pixie on *The Adventures of Ozzie and Harriet.* Even though it was just commercial work—and not a real part of the show—Mary was elated. All she had to do was put on a pixie costume and dance on a stove; the camera did the rest, reducing her to three inches on the screen so she really looked the part. Her single line of dialogue to Mrs. Nelson was no hardship, either: "Hi, Harriet. Aren't you glad you bought a Hotpoint?" Mary couldn't believe the job was actually hers. "All I had was moxie when I went into that audition," she recalls. "They gave me a script to read and I read it; they gave me a song to sing and I sang it—and that was that. When they told me I had the job, it was a high like nothing you could imagine."

After her first appearance, Hotpoint decided to sign her up as the show's permanent pixie. Her salary was $10,000 a year.

At the age of seventeen, Mary felt her career was suddenly starting to cook—thanks to Hotpoint appliances—and she could be as independent as she darn well pleased. With her new salary, she could rent her own apartment, buy a brand-new car, plan a trip to Europe during her time off from the show. She could move to the beach, fill her closets with all the latest fashions, make a whole new circle of friends. According to a lady in the wardrobe department, there was even a chance Mary could swing a date with David Nelson, Ozzie and Harriet's college-age son, if she played her cards right.

Instead, in August 1955—one month after going from high school to Hotpoint—Mary took her freedom and virtually threw it away. She married Richard Meeker, a twenty-eight-year-old salesman who lived next door to her parents. He was mature, considerate, dependable, and he had Marjorie Moore's seal of approval. (In fact, it was Mary's mom who had originally pushed the romance.) The trouble was that Mary—only seventeen—wasn't really ready to handle marriage, or the next step, motherhood, that came so soon afterward.

Why did she do it? Even today, after years of psychoanalysis and self-examination, Mary still has trouble explaining that early marriage. Did she hope Richard would be mature enough for the two of them? Perhaps.

"Getting married was the only way I could get out of the house legally," she once said. "I didn't want to go to college."

"I wanted to lead my own life," she remarked on another occasion. "A wedding band was my escape route. It was an out-and-out act of rebellion.

"I thought I was in love—and the only people who could have stopped me were my parents. But they were the last people in the world I would have listened to.

"Richard was so much older than me. He *was* ready for marriage. I thought he was ready enough for both of us."

In the fall of 1955—three months after they were married—Mary became pregnant. It wasn't exactly her original game plan, but Mary tried to be optimistic about things. True, morning sickness was hardly romantic, especially when she was trying to tap-dance on a stove and hide her pregnancy. But Mary wanted to make her marriage work. "I was young enough to believe that I could have it all—marriage, a baby, and a fabulous career," she once said. The first thing that happened was that her career went out the window.

It was simply impossible for her to be a pregnant pixie. Considering her well-rounded measurements—36–24–36—Mary never should have been a pixie in the first place, but she had managed to fool the camera—not to mention the director and the sponsor—by wearing a special binder that flattened her breasts. Pregnancy changed all that. It became impossible to hide her breasts, stomach, or hips. Never mind that her complexion sometimes turned green under the sweltering lights and that she was constantly fighting queasiness and fatigue. "The worst part was that my tummy was starting to pop right out of my skin-tight leotard," she recalls. "I looked ridiculous and they let me go."

Her son—Richard Carlton Meeker, Jr.—was born on July 3, 1956. Mary was only eighteen and a half years old. For better or worse, she was now both a wife and a mother with obligations and responsibilities to match. Her mother's pre-wedding advice still rang in her ears: "I think you're too young to get married, but if you and Dick ever separate, it'll be your fault and you'd better have a darn good reason."

Mary was working hard at her marriage, tackling homemaking and motherhood with the same dedication that she had previously given only to acting and dance. But she was slowly beginning to discover that, in relationships, practice doesn't always make perfect. She and Dick had serious differences that were becoming more and more apparent to her. Her husband was a real outdoorsman; he loved hunting, and Mary hated the sport—she always had. As a child, visiting her father's parents in Virginia, Mary had been sickened by the sight of stuffed birds and deer heads in her grandfather's trophy room. She simply could not deal with cruelty to animals in any way, shape, or form. Once, shortly after her family moved to Los Angeles, Mary saw a man beating his dog on the street; she ran right up to the man and kicked him.

Years later, when she became a celebrity spokeswoman for the prevention of cruelty to animals, she told *Good Housekeeping* how much she had been revolted by her husband's sporting attitude. Mary always refused to go hunting with him, but even their camping expeditions became a nightmare for her. "I won't ever forget how horrible I felt the first time I saw him shoot a rabbit," she said. "Here was this beautiful, lively little creature, who had been leaping about just moments before, lying dead and still—for no good reason! I burst into tears!"

In retrospect, Mary's absolute revulsion toward guns, indeed weapons of any kind, seems tragically prophetic. Her own son died by putting a gun near his head and accidentally pulling the trigger.

Richie's problems were still a long way off, though, when Mary decided to reactivate her career in the summer of 1957. Dick was now a sales representative for CBS, but simply being the wife of a junior television executive wasn't enough for Mary—not nearly enough. She desperately needed to be working, to be dancing, again. Whatever Dick's feelings on the subject might have been, he didn't try to stop her. Not that anybody could have. Mary, who had always been such a fiercely independent child, was proving to be just as formidable as a wife.

By the time of Richie's first birthday, she was back making the casting rounds. Before long, she was being hired to dress up the scenery on one variety show after another. In the late 1950s, variety shows, like westerns, were the meat and potatoes of TV programming and chorus dancers were a popular commodity. Mary looked good, danced well, and was blessed with an exquisite pair of legs. That combination was her ticket to success. She danced her way from George Gobel's show to Eddie Fisher's to Jimmy Durante's.

But then where? It very quickly dawned on her that a TV chorus line was a dead end. Singers and comediennes might be lucky enough to get their own shows, but dancers just finished out their careers in fishnet-stockinged anonymity. Their tap shoes might just as well have danced taps. There was nowhere to go. The movies didn't offer any magic answers, either.

"When I was a child, I had visions of myself dancing in a big studio musical," Mary often said, "but I realized very quickly that as long as Hollywood had four or five top dancers, there wasn't room for any more. They had Cyd Charisse, Mitzi Gaynor, Juliet Prowse, Barrie Chase—that's enough, they didn't need me."

Even in the best of times, Hollywood had groomed only one Ginger Rogers to every four or five Myrna Loys, but by 1957 Hollywood wasn't even bothering to make many musicals anymore. Just a few adaptations of big Broadway hits—and those roles always went to Shirley Jones, with one or two thrown to Mitzi Gaynor and Gwen Verdon. The era of the foxtrotting heroine and the tapdancer with moxie was on the way out. Shirley MacLaine—one of Broadway's most talented young dancers—was already making the switch into straight comedy and serious acting roles.

If Mary had been living in New York, Broadway might have been her salvation. In 1959, the musical comedy was still alive and kicking on the Great White Way with *The Sound of Music, Gypsy, Fiorello, Take Me Along, My Fair Lady,* and *The Music Man* all running at the same time. But unless she could phone in her performance, there was no way she could succeed on Broadway with or without really trying. She was married to a Californian. Her husband's work was in Los Angeles; he had no reason to want to uproot himself, so relocating in New York was out of the question. Mary had three choices: she could spend the rest of her life as the second girl from the right on "The Perry Como Christmas Special," run for president of the PTA—or figure out a professional route that made sense in LA.

Like a nervous contestant on *The Price Is Right,* Mary chose door number three. In her case, she didn't get a frost-free refrigerator or a weekend at the Desert Inn, just a hunch about what the right escape hatch might be from her dilemma. She decided she would *act.* Act? Why not? In Los Angeles, where television was the major industry, actors—not singers or dancers—were in demand. Very well, Mary Tyler Moore would learn to act. How difficult could it be? Although she'd never taken a single acting lesson— and didn't know Stanislavsky from Strasberg—Mary had no trouble putting together a résumé that made casting directors look twice. She simply invented all her acting credits.

"It wasn't very hard once I got the knack of it," she recalls. "I would just breeze through the door and when they asked about my background, I'd mention some obscure play that I'd done in Milwaukee or Chicago. It worked like a charm." Besides, Mary also had something else going for her: castability. She was blessed with a classic all-American face in an era when wholesomeness and home entertainment were almost synonymous.

But it was her legs, not her face, that first gave her TV visibility as an actress. She became Sam, the mysterious telephone operator who purred David Janssen's phone messages to him on "Richard Diamond: Private Detective." Mary had no idea what lay ahead when she auditioned for the part. All she knew was that the producers were looking for a girl with attractive legs, beautiful hands, and a throaty, sexy voice. Even though she washed her own dishes every night and had to train her voice to sound like Lauren Bacall, not her usual cheerleader self, Mary won the role over fifty other candidates.

In February 1959, when she reported on the set for the first time, she realized why no one had bothered to schedule her for hair styling or makeup. She could look like Godzilla from the waist up and it wouldn't matter. Sam was a gimmick on "Richard Diamond"; only her legs and hands would be visible as she answered the switchboard every week. The audience would never see her face or learn her real identity, since Mary would get no screen credit at the end of the show. She was there simply to create a fantasy, that's all. Americans could think Sam was anyone from Mae West to Marilyn Monroe to Mamie Eisenhower; the producers didn't care. In fact, the more people speculated about it, the more the ratings went up.

It was her first TV series, but for Mary it felt more like a part-time job. She never got to know David Janssen, since they never worked together; and Mary got so blasé about the role that sometimes she'd film her scenes with her hair still in curlers and her script propped up in front of her (well out of camera range). "Talk about phoning in your lines," she once joked, "on that show I really could have."

In May of 1959 *TV Guide* blew the whistle on the whole affair when Mary modeled women's hosiery for them. Later that month, she left the show in a contract dispute. Mary, who was earning $80 a show, wanted a raise; Dick Powell and Four Star Productions, who owned the show, said no. "There are lots of other girls out there with legs just as good as yours," they argued. But money was only part of the problem. Mary had been unhappy in the role from day one. Her scenes were mostly throwaway stuff; it was how she crossed her legs, not how she read her lines, that mattered. And she felt the role would do nothing for her professionally, since nobody knew she was on the show, anyway.

Ironically, Dick Powell did more for Mary than all the publicists in the world. All that secrecy generated tremendous public interest, and when she finally came out of the closet, so to speak, after thirteen weeks, Mary was something of an instant celebrity. No other cameo role could have done even half as much for her.

Her leaving (she was replaced by Roxanne Brooks) drew coverage in all the trade papers; and, as a result, Mary had no trouble getting offers for new jobs. From 1959 till the fall of 1961, when she became a permanent fixture on *The Dick Van Dyke Show*, Mary worked steadily, averaging five or six guest spots on dramatic shows each season. She did *Bourbon Street Beat*, *Johnny Staccato*, *77 Sunset Strip*, *The Millionaire*, *Wanted: Dead or Alive*, *Checkmate*, *Bachelor Father*, *The Deputy*, *The Aquanauts*, and three episodes of *Hawaiian Eye*. Mary invariably played the good girl or the good wife—she looked too wholesome to get away with anything else. "I was always cast as the long-suffering wife of some sort of juvenile delinquent," Mary once said.

Between her dramatic roles and variety-show stints, Mary appeared on sixty-five different shows. And she had a girl named Sam to thank for it all. "After I left *Richard Diamond*, casting directors started using me in roles because they felt it would be a coup to show the real 'Sam's' face," she once said.

In 1959 she almost became Danny Thomas's daughter Terry on *The Danny Thomas Show*, but her nose got in the way. Mary was a top contender to replace Sherry Jackson, who was leaving the show after five seasons. She auditioned several times for Danny Thomas and finally complained to her husband that "I wish I knew one way or the other because I'm so nervous each interview is costing me a can of deodorant."

Ultimately, the role went to Penny Parker, not Mary. The decision had nothing to do with either girl's sense of comedy or lack of it. It was a question of matching noses. Danny explained to Mary that her nose was too nondescript. "Honey, people just won't believe a girl like you could belong to me."

Mary joked back, "Listen, I'll have plastic surgery—I'll get a bump put on it."

Even though she still lost the role, it was the perfect parting shot. Somewhere in the back of his mind Danny Thomas remembered that the girl with the normal nose and three names was awfully cute and awfully funny.

Two years later, it paid off. Danny was supervising a new project for Desilu Studios—an off-beat comedy series about a TV comedy writer, starring Dick Van Dyke. Four days before the pilot was scheduled to be shot—after the producers had considered practically every available inge-nue from Elinor Donahue to Elizabeth Montgomery—the part of Dick's wife remained uncast. According to television legend, Danny Thomas and producer Sheldon Leonard were discussing the problem in Danny's Desilu office, while he was having his hair cut. They were reviewing their notes on a dozen or so actresses who seemed the most likely candidates so far, when Leonard finally said, "That's it. Can you think of any more?"

The word *more* jogged Danny's memory. He jumped out of his seat, almost knocked over the barber, and began screaming to his secretary for the Hollywood Players Di-rectory, so he could look up that girl "with the nice nose and three names."

Much later Danny wisecracked that Mary Tyler Moore owed him a haircut. At that point, Mary was so grateful for the audition that she probably would have thrown in a manicure and hot towel treatment, too. Besides, it was a lot cheaper than having plastic surgery, as she'd once volun-teered to do.

Although it was a whole generation before the term be-came popular, the casting of Mary Tyler Moore on *The Dick*

Van Dyke Show was definitely "high concept." From the beginning, she made Laura Petrie—the valiant young New Rochelle housewife—both heartwarming and hilarious. There was a touch of Camelot in teaming Dick Van Dyke with Mary Tyler Moore; the youthful image they projected was very like the appeal of the Kennedys in the White House. On the surface, both seemed like the perfect all-American couple.

Off-screen, Mary's private life was anything but Camelot. She hardly fit America's image of the perfect homemaker; she chain-smoked, hated cooking, and would have felt as out of place in a suburban coffee klatsch as a football player at a bridal shower. Starring on *The Dick Van Dyke Show* changed everything. She saw her five-year-old son for a few minutes every morning over breakfast, then spent an hour or two with him before bedtime. She and her husband Dick had almost nothing in common at this point. They were virtually strangers living under the same roof, albeit a rather expensive new roof. As a last-ditch effort to salvage their marriage, they had just bought a Spanish stucco house and were spending every weekend remodeling it. They knocked out walls themselves, stripped off wallpaper, broke through rooms, retiled the roof. The plan was to change the style of the house from pseudo-Spanish to French Regency. The renovation, like the marriage, somehow got sidetracked.

Through it all, the CBS publicity machine continued to churn out happy-actress/happy-wife copy. With a new comedy series to promote, it was imperative that Mary's off-screen image match Laura Petrie's snug-as-a-bug domesticity. That Christmas, while her marriage was already in tatters, Mary gave cheery press interviews about her favorite hobby—wrapping Christmas packages. Sometimes she'd spend an hour and a half decorating a single box. "I save odds and ends during the year—feathers, an earring that has lost its mate, the remains of a broken set of pearls. I get so involved in wrapping packages, I can spend hours doing it." She lamented that *The Dick Van Dyke Show* was cutting into her ribbon-cutting time. In 1961, she sent out 125 Christmas gifts, but only wrapped 20 herself, and even those she sloughed off, barely spending thirty minutes wrapping and decorating each one.

In a way, Mary's publicity that year was a sign of the times; for in 1961 America still belonged to Betty Crocker, not Betty Friedan. Had Mary been speaking in 1981, instead of 1961, she might have worried out loud about more significant matters: particularly her time away from her son. But in 1961 it wasn't safe to dwell on that. A television actress might not have time to wrap Christmas presents—that was acceptable—but she was expected to have time for her family, no matter how hard she worked.

In February 1962—five months after the premiere of *The Dick Van Dyke Show*—Mary quietly divorced Richard Meeker. But she didn't stay single for long. On June 1, 1962, she slipped away to Las Vegas to marry Grant Tinker at the Dunes Hotel. At the time he was an ad agency executive who represented one of the sponsors of *The Dick Van Dyke Show*. He was also the father of four children and newly divorced. The romance drew little public attention, since neither of them was a front-page news figure yet. *The Dick Van Dyke Show* was still foundering in the Tuesday-night ratings against *Laramie* and *Bachelor Father*; and Mary —the rookie of the cast—was overshadowed by more experienced zanies like Morey Amsterdam and Rose Marie. There was only a brief mention of her divorce in the papers. Later a few columnists noted that, while on a visit to New York, Mary was accompanied by Grant Tinker. They caught some Broadway shows together, including Barbara

Bel Geddes's comedy hit, *Mary, Mary,* and checked out "Twist King" Chubby Checkers's act at the Peppermint Lounge. Did Grant and Mary try the twist themselves? Only halfheartedly, the other patrons reported.

In 1974, Mary told a feature writer for *The New York Times Magazine* that she never felt guilty about walking away from her first marriage. "I'm sad if I made my husband unhappy by leaving," she said, "but life is too short not to live it fully." "Do you regret those years?" the interviewer asked. "I can't regret them," Mary replied. "I have Richie."

In essence, Mary and Richard Meeker were simply a mismatched couple—they wanted very different things out of life—but of course at the time Mary fell in love with him, she was too young to know it.

By the summer of 1962, Mary was twenty-four and a half years old and a little wiser—and much tougher. Her first season on *The Dick Van Dyke Show* had changed her. So had her divorce. No matter how lightly she brushed it off, Mary had disappointed her parents, upset her five-year-old son, and broken one of the basic doctrines of her faith. Before, whenever she had tried hard, she had always succeeded. Now she had failed at something. For a perfectionist, that's pretty hard to take.

❧ 2 ❧

First, You Laugh...

Some years they give Emmies to Latka's wife or the Bionic Woman, mainly because there are so few women's performances (outstanding or otherwise) to choose from. But the 1963–64 television season was an abundance of riches. Patty Duke was playing identical cousins—a Brooklyn Heights sweathog and a British swell—on her own situation comedy series, Shirley Booth was *Hazel*, Inger Stevens was *The Farmer's Daughter*, and Irene Ryan was Granny on *The Beverly Hillbillies*. On the dramatic front, Shirl Conway and Zina Bethune were giving Casey and Kildare a run for their stethoscopes as *The Nurses*.

But on May 25, 1964, the Emmy for Outstanding Continued Performance by an Actress in a Series (Lead) went to Mary Tyler Moore. After three seasons on *The Dick Van Dyke Show*, Mary had arrived. She was no longer just a "rookie" or a supporting player, she was a star. She'd never have to worry about getting a table at the Polo Lounge.

In her acceptance speech, Mary went out of her way to thank the show's creator, Carl Reiner, and the reason was obvious. He had not only created Laura Petrie, he had altered his original concept of the character considerably to showcase Mary's talents. Mary had been hired to play George Burns to Dick Van Dyke's Gracie Allen. But once the show got going, Reiner had relented and let the funny lady inside her come out.

Back in 1959, when Mary was still answering the phone on *Richard Diamond,* Carl Reiner was putting his phone on hold and turning away callers left and right. He was "hot," as they say, and everyone wanted him to play second fiddle to Andy Griffith or Richard Crenna in some goofy new sitcom, but Reiner wasn't interested. After seven years as Sid Caesar's TV sidekick on *Your Show of Shows* and *Caesar's Hour,* he wanted to do something more significant with his life. Since all the scripts that were being offered him seemed to have a nursery school mentality (this was the era of *McHale's Navy* and *The Beverly Hillbillies*), he decided to write his own series. After being an uncredited member of Sid Caesar's writing crew, and bumping typewriters with Neil Simon and Larry Gelbart, he felt confident about creating and selling his own show.

The idea he came up with was more than faintly autobiographical. Carl Reiner's show—tentatively titled *Head of the Family*—was the saga of a TV gag writer who lived with his wife and son in New Rochelle, New York. And New Rochelle just happened to be the Westchester suburb that Reiner called home. The main character, Rob Petrie, was named after Reiner's own son, Rob (who'd later skyrocket to fame on *All in the Family*), and the Petries' New Rochelle address—448 Bonnie Meadow Road—was just a few digits away from the real Reiner residence.

Peter Lawford, who'd just finished up starring on TV as *The Thin Man* for two years, agreed to produce the project and even got some financial backing from his famous father-in-law, Joseph Kennedy. The pilot was shot in New York with a cast that bore little resemblance to the stars of the final version. Reiner himself played Rob Petrie and a blond actress named Barbara Britton was the first Laura.

She probably would have made a better leading lady for Peter Lawford, since detective dramas were also her forte. In her last TV series, *Mr. and Mrs. North*, she'd played a crime hunter's wife in real Nora Charles fashion.

A child actor named Gary Morgan was the Petries' original son Ritchie and Morty Gunty was wisecracking Buddy Sorrell. As for the first Sally Rogers—an unknown named Sylvia Miles—she found success in films nearly ten years later. She won Oscar nominations for *Midnight Cowboy* (1969) and *Farewell, My Lovely* (1975) although she didn't get many laughs in either movie.

The pilot aired on CBS's *Comedy Spot*—the show that took over for Red Skelton every summer—but *Head of the Family* didn't make it onto the fall 1960 lineup. Peter Lawford dropped out as producer, and that's when Danny Thomas and his business partner, Sheldon Leonard, came into the picture. After reading the thirteen weekly scripts that Carl Reiner had already written, they were convinced that *Head of the Family* could succeed. They just didn't think that Reiner could succeed as the head of the family, so they convinced him to take an occasional guest-starring role as Alan Brady (the star of the show Rob wrote for) and to let them find a new Rob Petrie.

The choice narrowed down to two up-and-coming actors —Johnny Carson and Dick Van Dyke. The scales tipped in favor of Van Dyke after the producers caught his Tony-winning performance in the Broadway musical *Bye Bye Birdie*, and they quickly signed him to a five-year contract with a $1,500-a-show starting salary.

Mary Tyler Moore, of course, wasn't cast until the revised pilot was almost ready to be shot for CBS (this time in LA) and her starting salary was a lot lower than Van Dyke's. Morey Amsterdam and Rose Marie, both TV, radio, and nightclub veterans, were signed up much more quickly, and Richard Deacon, who'd been a semi-regular on *Leave It to Beaver,* became Rob Petrie's oafish boss, Mel Cooley. Larry Mathews took over as Ritchie.

The New York pilot had hinged on a father-and-son theme: Rob brings Ritchie to his office to meet Buddy and Sally, his fellow gag makers, and to see what comedy writers do all day. Sheldon Leonard wanted a whole new angle for the LA pilot. In the script that was chosen, Rob and Laura have to attend one of Alan Brady's parties. They leave Ritchie with a baby-sitter, but Laura can't relax at the party because she's sure Ritchie is coming down with a cold. And, in typical situation-comedy style, it all goes downhill from there.

That pilot, which became the show's very first episode on October 3, 1961, immediately moved Mary Tyler Moore to the center of the stage and she surprised all the show's veterans by holding her own in every scene. Carl Reiner was so inspired by Mary's performance that he began writing whole episodes focused upon Laura. The second show, which aired on October 10, was called "My Blonde-Haired Brunette" and dealt with Laura's hilarious attempt to go platinum as a turn-on for her uninterested husband. During the show's first season, Laura also matched up Sally with a druggist, suspected Rob of having an affair, resumed her dancing career, and dealt with everything from an ugly jewelry gift to an unwelcome dog.

Mary was ranked a notch below Dick Van Dyke in the eyes of the producers and the public. She may have gotten more than a fair shake in the scripts, but it was Dick's show, and not in name only. As the years went on and her success grew, Mary found it harder and harder to settle for supporting-player status.

In the beginning, though, they all felt lucky just to be on the air. In the fall of 1961, comedies about love and marriage weren't generating much excitement at the networks. Action shows were what everybody wanted. The big ratings-grabbers were westerns—*Gunsmoke, Wagon Train, Rawhide* —and hip detective yarns like *77 Sunset Strip*. It had taken a lot of arm-twisting on the part of Danny Thomas and Sheldon Leonard to line up some sponsors—Procter & Gamble and General Foods, for starters—and to get CBS to back *Dick Van Dyke* at all.

At first, the network's reluctance seemed vindicated. *Dick Van Dyke* hardly made a dent in the ratings. After a faltering half season on the air, CBS moved the show from a Tuesday- to a Wednesday-night time shot, but ratings barely improved. That spring it looked as if the show might not even be renewed. In March, CBS released its tentative new lineup for the fall of 1962 and *The Dick Van Dyke Show* was conspicuously missing.

"For a few days there, we were canceled," Dick later admitted to *Variety* columnist Dave Kaufman. But a savior named Nick Keesely came along at the eleventh hour. Keesely was an executive at Lorillard, which already sponsored *The Joey Bishop Show*, and Keesely happened to be a Dick Van Dyke fan. Through his influence, Lorillard agreed to pick up half the sponsorship for the fall 1962 season (P&G would retain the other half), and at the same time Sheldon Leonard went to CBS corporate headquarters in New York to plead for a reprieve. "He convinced them it was worth saving," Dick Van Dyke recalls. "We had all given up. There was a lot of disappointment for reasons above the loss of income and steady jobs. The chemistry between the people involved—Rose Marie, Mary Tyler Moore, Morey Amsterdam, and myself—was great; we all liked each other."

Finally, CBS relented and *Dick Van Dyke* got a second chance. Summer helped, and people who hadn't tuned in the first time got hooked on Rob and Laura Petrie et al. when reruns started. Most of them decided to stick with *Dick Van Dyke* in the fall. CBS also decided to put the show on right after *The Beverly Hillbillies* on Wednesday night— and before long *Dick Van Dyke* was doing an incredible flip-flop in the Nielsens. In April 1962, *The Dick Van Dyke Show* finished in ninth place for the year—ahead of both *Gunsmoke* and *Dr. Kildare.* By the third season, *Dick Van Dyke* had become a Wednesday-night institution. It was now the third most popular television series in America. Only *The Beverly Hillbillies* and *Gunsmoke* drew bigger Nielsen numbers.

But in the last analysis it wasn't clever programming ploys that made *The Dick Van Dyke Show* catch on. It was the show's own special brand of charm. Here was a situation comedy with style and wit—and restraint, too. *Dick Van Dyke* was wise enough never to parody the worlds it peeked into. Life in the Westchester suburbs and life behind the scenes at *The Alan Brady Show*—both of those settings could have provided abundant material for put-downs and pot-shots, but *Dick Van Dyke* always remembered it was a sit-com, not a satire, and so we cared about the characters, even while we laughed. And, of course, our hero and heroine, Rob and Laura Petrie, kept us down to earth. They completely defied all of Sinclair Lewis's theories about ordinary Americans: everyday people *don't* have to be boring. Perhaps the most refreshing change of all was the delightful chemistry that existed between Rob and Laura—that was definitely something new in the world of TV comedy. For the first time, viewers had the distinct impression that more went on in this marriage than just an occasional goodnight kiss wafted between twin beds.

Their relationship—close and warm and loving—became the backbone of the show, and it brought TV comedy into the 1960s with a healthy bang. Yet why wasn't a more romantic title chosen? *The Dick Van Dyke Show* certainly didn't advertise the marital aspect of the comedy. Actually, after CBS had nixed the first pilot, *Head of the Family*, Reiner and company had kicked around a few other titles —*Double Trouble*, *Two Loves Have I*, and *Mommy! Daddy's Home*—but they all sounded too dull, too cute, or too much like a soap opera. Eventually, Reiner and CBS settled on *The Dick Van Dyke Show*. They figured that if the show was a hit, that's what everyone would wind up calling it anyway. Few people remembered that *The Phil Silvers Show* started out as *You'll Never Get Rich* and *The Danny Thomas Show* was first called *Make Room for Daddy*.

Having the series named after him put Dick in a peculiar position. If the show had failed, it would have been harder for him to make people forget his association with it; by the same token, once it succeeded, Dick got the lion's share of the attention.

Dick tried to be self-effacing about it all. Despite the fact that *Bye Bye Birdie* (with Ann-Margret) and *Mary Poppins* (with Julie Andrews) had turned him into a movie star as well as a TV idol, Dick told magazine writer C. Robert Jennings that he didn't think of himself as a Hollywood celebrity. He felt that distinction belonged to Cary Grant and Fred Astaire—not to guys like Dick Van Dyke. Jennings summed up Van Dyke's image of himself as "a second banana—the man they send for when Jack Lemmon is unavailable."

Well, if Dick Van Dyke only qualified as a second banana, what did that make Mary Tyler Moore? Whatever her status was, it certainly wasn't Dick's equal. In a sense, it was the title of the show that placed her at a disadvantage. Any husband-and-wife comedy series is really a two-star situation—think of Lucy and Desi or Burns and Allen—

but in this case the show's title immediately implied that Dick Van Dyke—the star—was the comic and Mary was just a very pretty straight man in Capri pants. Suddenly she had a pretty good idea how Carl Betz must have felt on *The Donna Reed Show*. But Mary was wise enough to realize she had nothing to complain about. This was her first TV series—if you didn't count her leggy interlude on *Richard Diamond*—so she was hardly in a "supporting player" rut yet.

Still, there were times when the situation must have rankled, especially since Rose Marie—who was the show's resident second banana—somehow projected an air of being on par with Mary, whom she viewed as an inexperienced ingenue. Rose Marie had been in show business practically since birth and she wasn't shy about advertising it. She even had a sign tacked up on her dressing room door: FORMER CHILD STAR. "Could you ever imagine Vivian Vance trying that on Lucy's show?" a stagehand once remarked. "She would have been out of there on her you-know-what."

At first there was a real sense of friction between Mary, the novice, and Rose Marie, the old pro. But in time their hostility mellowed, and while they never became bosom buddies off screen, they were more than willing to acknowledge each other's strengths and contributions to the show. Rose Marie had to admit that Mary's instincts as a comedienne were beyond question. When Mary watched Rose Marie work, she couldn't deny the fact that she was in the presence of a master. No matter how brusque Rose Marie might be with her, here was a woman who could teach a young actress an awful lot about comedy. They couldn't help but respect each other's talent, and that drew them together.

Off the set, Mary's closest pal was Ann Morgan Guilbert, who played Laura's neighbor, Millie Helper. During rehearsal breaks, Ann and Mary would organize marathon word-game competitions and corral other cast and crew members into joining them. "I was really close to Ann when we were doing the show," Mary recalls. "I liked her a lot. We were the Perquacky champions."

The weekly rehearsal cycle began on Wednesday morning when the cast got together to read the script for the first time. The rehearsal table, which someone had dubbed "The Christian Science Reading Room," was always stocked with plenty of coffee and doughnuts when Mary, Dick, and the rest of the gang arrived. The rehearsal call was for ten A.M., but Sheldon Leonard always allowed the gang a full hour just to kibitz before they really got down to business.

Each actor had two scripts in front of him: a final, white-copy draft of that week's script, and a rough, pink-copy draft of the script they'd be working on the week after. On Wednesday they always did a quick reading of the pink script first, so they could get a general idea of what might be wrong with it, if anything, and send it back to the writers with requests for revisions.

After that, the cast concentrated only on the white script —that week's show. They rehearsed Wednesday, Thursday, and Friday, then broke for the weekend. But changes were still being made. On Saturday, messengers delivered revised pages of dialogue to the actors' homes so the actors could learn their new lines for Monday. At the Monday run-through, the director blocked out everybody's moves on camera—and Tuesday was opening night. That day the cast didn't arrive till noon, when makeup and wardrobe were the first priorities. After a preliminary camera run-through, there was dress rehearsal in front of the producers, who had more notes and comments for the actors. Then, around six P.M., the cast broke for dinner. At seven-thirty P.M. the show was filmed before a live audience.

Aside from the eight regulars—Dick Van Dyke, Mary Tyler Moore, Morey Amsterdam, Rose Marie, Larry Mathews, Richard Deacon, Ann Morgan Guilbert, and Jerry Paris (Millie's husband)—the guest list was a miniature who's who in Hollywood. Future *M*A*S*H* star Jamie Farr played a delivery boy in several early episodes. Vic Damone was cast as a swinging singer, Rick Vallone, who turned cynical Sally into a quivering bowl of Jello. Don Rickles played Lyle Delp, the hold-up man who got trapped in an elevator with Rob and Laura, then reappeared when the Petries put on a musical show at his prison. Stacy Keach was a doctor, Ed Begley was a judge, and Marty Ingels was Rob's old Army buddy, Sol Pomeroy. Dick's brother, Jerry Van Dyke, occasionally played Rob's sleepwalking brother, Stacey Petrie, and Carl Reiner had several incarnations as neurotic TV star Alan Brady, mad painter Serge Carpetna, and literary snob Yale Sampson, among others. Even Danny Thomas and Sheldon Leonard managed to sneak in front of the *Dick Van Dyke* cameras every now and then.

Every character on the show had a personal trademark. Mary made Capri pants and bangs popular, Dick brought living-room ottomans into national prominence, and, in a wacky way, Richard Deacon gave new stature to baldness. But despite its rich sense of characterization and 1960s sophistication (one episode called "That's My Boy" had racial overtones and almost didn't get on the air), many critics saw *Dick Van Dyke* as simply an updated version of *I Love Lucy*. Both were basically two-couple comedies. And Laura Petrie definitely had a lot of Lucy in her. She was always getting into ridiculous scrapes that drove her husband wild, but invariably they'd kiss and make up by the end of the episode. When Laura got her foot caught in the bathroom drain in a swanky hotel, shades of Lucy were everywhere.

There were other similarities, too. Like the Ricardos, the Petries had a single child—in both cases it was a boy—and always got into their best comedy jams in tandem with another couple who were even slower on the uptake than they were. Lucy and Ricky, of course, never made a move without the assistance of their slightly befuddled neighbors, Fred and Ethel Mertz. While the Petries also had a pair of neighbors—Dr. Jerry Helper and his wife, Millie— who sometimes served this purpose, their real partners in lunacy were Rob's writing associates, Sally Rogers and Buddy Sorrell. Remember how Fred and Ethel seemed to spend more time in Lucy's apartment than in their own? Well, on *Dick Van Dyke*, Buddy and Sally were practically live-in friends. Rob and Laura were so umbilically bound with them that Buddy seemed to spend more time in New Rochelle than he did at home with his wife Pickles.

The very fact that Rob, Buddy, and Sally all worked on *The Alan Brady Show* echoed *I Love Lucy*, too. Ricky, after all, had been a nightclub bandleader, and Lucy's recurring attempts to break into show business herself provided a lot of laughs. Laura's often ingenuous style of "talk first, think later" frequently got Rob in trouble at work, too—like the time she publicly announced that Alan Brady wore a toupee. And Laura's own show-business ambitions (she was a talented dancer who'd given up her career to marry Rob), like Lucy's, always came to naught. Apparently it was okay for American housewives to have starstruck fantasies as long as they stayed safely in New Rochelle—a very long forty-five minutes from Broadway.

Rob Petrie, like Ricky Ricardo, was outstanding husband material. He adored his family, never fooled around, and was always understanding enough to forgive his wife's wacky lapses. As for Buddy and Sally, although they were never romantically involved, their relationship was practically a replica of Fred and Ethel's marriage. They were substantially older than the Petries (just as the Mertzes were older than the Ricardos), but no wiser for all their extra years; and they needled each other mercilessly—just like any other middle-aged married couple.

But Laura and Lucy had the closest kinship of all. They both wept a lot, had difficulty operating appliances, made crazy snap decisions that they always regretted (like Laura dying her hair blonde), and had a great facility for embarrassing their husbands at work. More significantly, neither wife worked, nor ever wandered very far afield from her own safe little enclave. Lucy's world was her New York City apartment building, Laura's her New Rochelle split. Lucy couldn't cope more than two blocks from home and Laura never felt comfortable visiting Rob's office in Manhattan.

Judging by later, more liberated standards, Laura seems something of a suburban cliché. While Rob ran for a city council post in one episode—and worked on a cultural documentary program in another—Laura's concerns rarely rose above the mundane. She fretted over scratches on their brand-new car and saw marital Armageddon every time a pretty woman entered Rob's working life. Still and all, even if independence wasn't her strong suit, she wasn't exactly Harriet Nelson, either. Right from the start, Mary surprised everyone by getting a laugh every chance she got. She made Laura far funnier than the passive character Carl Reiner had originally intended her to be. She'd never had a comedy lesson in her life, but Mary was a born comedienne. First of all, she knew how to *listen* in a scene, which gave her a sense of timing. Secondly, she knew how to play down-to-earth without playing dumb. When Mary first au-

ditioned for the part, Carl Reiner was struck by her natu-
ralness. "She says hello like a real person, not like an actress," he went around telling everyone.

As soon as she was cast, Reiner and his staff started
inventing funny stuff for Mary. "It was obvious from the
first," Reiner told *TV Guide*, "that we had accidentally
stumbled on a kid of twenty-three who could do comedy."
Director John Rich echoed his sentiments, calling Mary's
comic sense "infallible." The sequence of shows was
shifted around to spotlight her character. The peroxide-
blonde episode—"My Blonde-Haired Brunette"—was the
ninth episode filmed, but it was aired a week after the show
debuted. The producer thought it had a better chance of
hooking viewers than some of the shows that focused on
Rob's work situation.

It soon became obvious that, except for salary and billing, Mary Tyler Moore was Dick Van Dyke's equal in
every way. Carl Reiner later said, "If you watch the early
Van Dyke shows, her development is apparent almost from
week to week. She knows where the jokes are. . . . She's a
fine comic actress. She has a fine instrument, as many dancers do [an interesting comparison in Mary's case], and she
knows how to use it." Reiner believed it was her vulnerabil-
ity that made Laura both terribly funny and touchingly
real. All through those five years, Reiner remained Mary
Tyler Moore's supporter—allowing Mary to hone her acting skills—and she only turned on him once. It was a 1965
script called "Never Bathe on Saturday"—the one where
Laura spends an entire weekend stuck in a bathtub. Most
Van Dyke aficionados consider that episode a classic, but
Mary was livid while filming it. When Reiner was working
on the script, he kept assuring Mary that each scene was
funnier than the one before it and all the funny business
had to do with Laura. Reiner didn't lie: the plot was hyster-

ical and Laura was the spark behind all the action. The only trouble was that most of the time she was off-screen, trapped in the tub, while Dick Van Dyke got all the laughs.

But one blowup in five years certainly doesn't qualify as temperamental behavior. Generally, whether she was happy or not, Mary kept quiet, did her work, and remained the "good team player." This was already becoming part of her image. It simply wasn't Mary's style to make waves— and never would be. Mary preferred to leave the decision making in the (hopefully capable) hands of her producers and directors. In the case of *The Dick Van Dyke Show*, it worked beautifully. Everything Carl Reiner, Sheldon Leonard, and John Rich did was ultimately in Mary's best interests.

For Mary, *The Dick Van Dyke Show* was more than a five-year trip in candyland, it was the most intensive learning period of her life—in a sense, the college education she never had. Mary had no illusions about her success. She knew she wasn't better than her material—not yet. She felt she succeeded on the show partly because the whole team was operating on a creative high. This cast was talent and experience personified. Occasionally that could be frightening to Mary; most of the time it was simply electrifying. "They were so good, I had to be good also just to keep up with them," she later explained. "Spending five years working with Dick Van Dyke, Morey Amsterdam, Rose Marie, Carl Reiner, and Sheldon Leonard—it was better than winning a scholarship to Actors Studio!"

Mary not only got free acting lessons, she even earned a diploma of sorts—her two Emmy trophies. In the 1962–63 season, both Mary and Dick were nominated for Emmies in the leading actor categories, but lost to Shirley Booth (*Hazel*) and E. G. Marshall (*The Defenders*), respectively. A year later, they both won, and this time Mary defeated

Shirley Booth, Patty Duke, Irene Ryan, and Inger Stevens. Two years later—on May 22, 1966—Mary garnered her second Emmy, as best actress in a leading role in a comedy series. This time she was no longer competing against actresses in serious dramatic roles, but the other two contenders, Lucille Ball (*The Lucy Show*) and Elizabeth Montgomery (*Bewitched*), were hardly lightweights. That same season—the show's last on the air—Dick Van Dyke took home his third Emmy, and for the fourth successive year the show was named Outstanding Comedy Series by the TV Academy voters.

Mary's two Emmies took up a place of honor in the house she now shared with Grant Tinker. Beside them stood her Golden Globe Award as 1964's Best Female Television Star.

Perhaps, for Mary, the best thing about the show was the family atmosphere. Carl Reiner was a family man—so was Dick Van Dyke—and the show tended to be accommodating about temporary interruptions due to personal difficulties. "If Mary wanted time off to take her son to the dentist, we rehearsed around her," a crew member recalls. Furthermore, kids were always welcome on the set, and Mary's son Richie, who was almost ten years old by the time *Dick Van Dyke* ended, was a frequent backstage visitor.

One of Dick Van Dyke's biggest admirers was Mary herself. They rarely exchanged a harsh word during five years of working together. Of course, like Mary, Dick was not a person who expressed his anger easily. "That smile covers up everything," Carl Reiner once remarked. "He loses his temper, but you never know it—he goes quietly into his room and stews and makes you think he is just going to the bathroom."

Rose Marie has a slightly different perspective on the man. "Dick Van Dyke has *gotta* be a saint," she once said.

"There's just nobody like him. If the world was full of Dick Van Dykes, there'd be no more wars or hatred, just love and understanding. He's a beautiful husband and father. He'll call you up on a Saturday night and say, 'Hey, Marj and I are just sitting here by the fire, talking. Why don't you come on over?' "

Of course he had his problems, too, even though he kept them inside. The pressure of being the show's star—of feeling responsible for everything—occasionally got to him. On one side was the Dick Van Dyke that everyone, viewers and castmates alike, saw: likable, easygoing, Hollywood's first G-rated movie idol since Pat Boone, teaching Sunday school at the Brentwood Presbyterian Church. On the other side was the Dick Van Dyke who completely demolished his Jaguar speeding around a bend on Sunset Boulevard. Much later on, in the 1970s, Dick's all-American image took an even fiercer beating than his Jaguar when his long-time perfect marriage broke up and Dick made a public confession about his struggles with alcohol.

But all that was in the future. During the *Dick Van Dyke* years, few people—including Mary—suspected that Dick's grip on his home life and career wasn't as firm as everyone believed. His style of stardom was exactly what Mary set out to emulate when she launched her own show in 1970. Like Dick, she tried not to stand out as the star, but rather encouraged the cast to grow into an ensemble group of half a dozen strong performers. Teamwork, not temperament, was the valuable lesson Mary had learned from Dick Van Dyke, and it became a personal commandment in her own career.

Amazingly, Mary was the only cast member to achieve even greater stardom after the show folded. For the others, *The Dick Van Dyke Show* turned out to be the zenith itself, not a prelude to greater success. Dick Van Dyke's career sputtered and stalled all through the 1970s. After *Mary Poppins* and *Chitty Chitty Bang Bang*, his film career dwindled. His second attempt at a sitcom, *The New Dick Van Dyke Show*, hardly matched the style and wit of his Rob Petrie years; and his later Broadway comeback, in a revival of *The Music Man*, was a failure of disastrous proportions. His one notable triumph was in the CBS-TV movie *The Morning After*, in which Dick won an Emmy nomination for his portrayal of an alcoholic.

Rose Marie was Doris Day's TV sidekick for a while, but spent most of her time as a panelist on *Hollywood Squares*. Morey Amsterdam has hardly made any TV appearances at all, instead doing featured roles in forgettable films and making nightclub appearances. Richard Deacon's later series, *The Mothers-in-Law*, got shafted by NBC after two seasons, while Larry Mathews—the Petries' TV son—simply grew up and went to UCLA. Actually, Jerry Paris is probably the most successful graduate of *Dick Van Dyke* aside from Mary. Although his acting career never amounted to much after his performance as the star dentist of Bonnie Meadow Road, Jerry went on to produce and direct *Happy Days* for ten years. He also created the Robin Williams series *Mork and Mindy*.

Occasionally there have been reunions—some painful, some merely nostalgic. In 1969, Dick and Mary teamed up in a CBS variety special that took the ratings by storm. Eleven years later, they touched base once again, but in far different circumstances, when Dick was among those comforting Mary after the death of her son, Richie Meeker.

Larry Mathews recalls running into Dick Van Dyke on the street not long ago. "When Dick saw me, he said, 'The last time I saw you you were short and cute! What happened?' Then we both laughed," Larry remembers.

The fact is that for five years the *Dick Van Dyke* cast was a family, and no matter how far apart they may have drifted afterward, there's still a sense of fellowship underneath it all. They shared too many doughnuts and too many triumphs to ever forget. They crossed their fingers and hoped against hope when the show was almost canceled in 1962. Later, they cheered and got happily hoarse together each time the show won an Emmy—and they wept together when the last episode was filmed on March 22, 1966. It was the end of a very exciting era. Mary cried, too, even though she had pretty much kept to herself during those five years, rarely socializing with any of the cast or crew away from the studio. She only invited the gang to her house once, and then nearly died of embarrassment when the dinner didn't come out right (Mary's party anxieties, a very real part of her life, later became a recurring source of comedy on *The Mary Tyler Moore Show*).

After going through the paces of 158 scripts together, Mary was still an enigma to most of her castmates. Was she cold—or merely shy? She spent a great deal of her time in her dressing room, locked away from the others, but then again she had hairdo and makeup to take care of, not to mention wardrobe fittings. Actors are generally more available than actresses during rehearsal breaks, since they have less "getting ready" to do. But even when Mary did make an attempt at backstage camaraderie, it was usually to play Scrabble or sing a few songs at the piano. She never sought people out to pour out her problems or ask for personal advice. Everyone assumed Mary's life was always on an even keel, for she never gave them reason to suspect otherwise. Most of the cast learned that Mary was divorcing Richard Meeker when they read about it in the paper. Few of them had even known she had serious marital difficulties.

Richard Deacon later commented that Mary's inner determination was what kept her apart from everyone. It was like a plastic shield. On the set, she was pleasant, accommodating, and very eager to learn—but always aloof. "You love Mary, everybody does," Deacon said. "But you never know her beyond a certain point."

Five years later, Mary became the star of her own series, playing a character who was far more liberated than Laura Petrie. But in a strange way the fictional Mary Richards of 1970 was living through a lot of what the real Mary Tyler Moore had endured in 1961. It often seemed that some of the themes of *The Mary Tyler Moore Show* were reverberations of Mary's own past, as though the WJM newsroom was modeled after the Desilu Studios, where *The Dick Van Dyke Show* had filmed. In the *MTM* scenario, Mary Richards was a newcomer in a high-pressure job, trying to prove to a gruff but fatherly boss (shades of Carl Reiner and Sheldon Leonard?) that she could carry her own weight. Like Mary on *The Dick Van Dyke Show*, Mary Richards was surrounded on all sides by veterans radiating experience and impatience. At first she is slightly appalled by their quirks— Lou's insensitivity, Ted's ego, Murray's indecisivenesss— but gradually she grows to love them, and to learn from them, just as the real Mary did back on *DVD*.

But it was a long jump from New Rochelle to Minneapolis, and Mary nearly lost her footing on a few of the steps in between. At the time, she may not have realized just how sheltering an atmosphere *The Dick Van Dyke Show* had been. Now she was on her own for better or for worse.

In 1966, less than a year after *Dick Van Dyke* ended, Mary was in New York rehearsing for her Broadway debut. Leaving the Mark Hellinger Theatre on West Fifty-first Street alone, even in broad daylight, she was a little frightened. There were so many muggings in the theater district. Actually, nobody ever tried to snatch Mary's purse or grab her jewelry as she walked the West Side streets. But the beating she took inside the theater was far, far worse.

≫ 3 ≪

... Then You Cry

When *The Dick Van Dyke Show* came to a close, Mary decided it was time to put television behind her. Everywhere she looked she saw the same thing happening: all the charismatic young stars—Richard Chamberlain, James Garner, Connie Stevens, and Dorothy Provine, to mention just a few—were escaping from prime-time captivity as fast as they could and making the switch to movies. Obviously, it was the only way to go. In fact, Mary didn't have to look farther than her own leading man, Dick Van Dyke, to know what direction to take. On the heels of his 1964 success in *Mary Poppins*—a film he'd tossed off without much ado during a between-seasons TV break—Dick was signed to do another Walt Disney children's movie, *Chitty Chitty Bang Bang,* and at the same time was starring in *Divorce American Style,* a very adult comedy with Debbie Reynolds and Jason Robards, Jr.

To Mary, the land of movie-making looked equally green; and in the spring of 1966—surrounded by a small circle of lawyers, agents, film executives, and her husband, Grant Tinker—Mary was blissfully wedded to the world of Technicolor dreams. She signed a ten-picture contract with Universal Studios with a guarantee of $100,000 per picture. If Mary actually made all ten pictures, it would amount to a million-dollar deal.

Her first assignment—*Thoroughly Modern Millie*—seemed like a waste of Mary's talents, but she jumped at the chance to do it. *Millie* was a big-budget musical—a real throwback to the days of Dick Powell and Ruby Keeler—so how could an old movie musical lover like Mary resist? It was just the kind of thing she'd been fantasizing about doing all her life. And look at the people she'd be working with—Julie Andrews, Carol Channing, Bea Lillie—some of the greatest names in musical-theater history. Not to mention a score that included three new numbers by Sammy Cahn and Jimmy Van Heusen plus a liberal dose of 1920s classics like George Gershwin's "Do It Again." Of course, Julie Andrews was the undisputed star of this gaudy extravaganza —but so what? If Mary had to play second fiddle in her first motion-picture outing, she could live with that. Certainly in a film that size, Mary would have a few shining moments of her own.

Well, not necessarily. The trouble was that Julie Andrews and Mary Tyler Moore were both too wholesome to play well against each other. It was kind of like watching two Cindy Williamses and no Penny Marshall—so Julie's character wound up dominating the film, and Mary's was somehow lost in the shuffle. Julie—the star—got everything: the title role, top billing, a script that was tailor-made for her (to duplicate her Broadway success in *The Boyfriend*), the best dressing trailer, and practically every song in the production. Julie's syrupy soprano dominated nearly the entire 138 minutes of the film. She sang "Thoroughly Modern Millie," "The Tapioca," "Jimmy," "Baby Face," "Poor Butterfly," and "The Jewish Wedding Song." Mary had to settle for a single duet with Julie on a tune called "Stumbling." It was simply a case of clout, that's all. Mary may have had two Emmies to her credit, but those were just television trophies. She was no match for Oscar-winning Julie, who had broken box-office records in *Mary Poppins* and *The Sound of Music.* On top of that, Julie was on a first-name basis with *Thoroughly Modern Millie's* director, George Roy Hill, who had been her boss on *Hawaii* just the year before. Through it all, Mary at least had one consolation: if *Thoroughly Modern Millie* turned out to be even half the hit that everyone was predicting, her motion picture career would be off to a flying start.

In that sense, *Thoroughly Modern Millie* didn't disappoint her. When it opened in New York on March 21, 1967, it seemed like the perfect antidote to all our woes and worries —and audiences loved it even if the critics didn't. In a year when films like *The Graduate, Cool Hand Luke,* and *Bonnie and Clyde* were taking serious social stock of America— when Vietnam, civil rights riots, and campus protests filled the news—*Thoroughly Modern Millie* seemed to have been designed by producer Ross Hunter as a giant panacea for all our national ills. It was mindless, meaningless entertainment at its best (or its worst, depending on your point of view).

Millie was set in the Roaring Twenties—the most carefree, pleasure-seeking decade in American history. The story was simple, rather silly, and appropriately melodramatic: Millie Dillmount (Julie Andrews), a secretary turned flapper, befriended an orphaned heiress named Dorothy Brown (Mary Tyler Moore) and eventually saved her from captivity by a vicious white slaver (Beatrice Lillie). In the end, as a reward for her troubles, Millie waltzed off with a passionate paper-clip salesman (James Fox) and Dorothy married another white-collar Romeo (John Gavin).

As it turned out, *Thoroughly Modern Millie* was a triumph for everybody concerned—except for Mary. For Julie Andrews, it represented a comeback of sorts after two lacklus-

ter films in a row (*Hawaii, Torn Curtain*). For Carol Channing—who played Muzzy Von Hossmere—*Millie* proved
to be even more of a vindication. After immortalizing
Dolly Levi on Broadway, she had recently lost the screen
version of *Hello, Dolly!* to Barbra Streisand. But Carol made
up for the slight a bit by garnering a supporting-actress
Oscar nomination for her marvelous, zany work in *Millie*.

Sammy Cahn and Jimmy Van Heusen were also Academy Award contenders that year—for *Millie*'s title song—
and George Roy Hill was picked to direct an even bigger
plum, *Butch Cassidy and the Sundance Kid*, on the basis of his
success with *Millie*. Bea Lillie, of course, didn't have to
worry about success or failure—she was already an international legend. And producer Ross Hunter came out ahead
of everyone. Although Julie Andrews had begged him to
shorten the film and take out some of the excess sentimental
baggage in the script (like the "Jewish Wedding Song"
number) Hunter refused to budge—and, at least as far as
box-office receipts went, he may have known best.
Thoroughly Modern Millie drew in record crowds during its
Easter-week opening in 1967 and went on to become one of
Universal's all-time top money-makers.

Somehow, only Mary Tyler Moore got lost in the flap.
Since Julie dominated the film, Mary's performance garnered only a small mention in most reviews. The film's
funniest moments belonged to Carol Channing and Bea
Lillie; and Mary's screen presence wavered between wishy
and washy—a terrible omen, unfortunately, of things to
come. What Mary lacked was an ability to transform herself into an intriguing screen persona and develop it in film
after film. Without that identity, she'd never become a star.
All great screen performers have it; moviegoers immediately think of Paul Newman as the rebellious antihero, Jane
Fonda as feisty and independent, and Barbra Streisand as

the ugly duckling struggling to turn into a swan. But in her first film, Mary Tyler Moore failed to elicit that kind of connected response. Dorothy Brown wasn't much of anything except sweet—and while sweetness may be a premium commodity when it comes to candy, it's hardly a unique or memorable trait in an aspiring actress.

Worse yet, after *Thoroughly Modern Millie*, Mary continued to make films that stretched her sweetness quotient to a saccharine extreme. In *What's So Bad about Feeling Good?* — where even the title's play on words screamed "Cute" —Mary played a woman who adopts a bird that can magically bring people happiness. In *Change of Habit*, she portrayed a nun who tames Elvis Presley and corrects speech defects in the barrio.

Why did sugar and spice roles become Mary's route to stardom? Laura Petrie was probably the culprit. On television, Mary had been successful as a wholesome, all-American, girl-next-door type, and Universal was anxious to capitalize on that image. Let Faye Dunaway play beautiful gun molls and Joanne Woodward handle the neurotic-spinster roles—they could get away with it. But don't try to tamper with Mary Tyler Moore's halo; her television fans wouldn't sit still for it. Unfortunately, none of the four films that Mary made from 1966 to 1969 was anywhere near as well written as her *Dick Van Dyke* scripts. Hollywood tried to keep her Laura Petrie forever—and nearly froze her career in the process.

Only once did Mary try to break out of her good-girl mold—when she agreed to play Holly Golightly, the $50-a-night girl in *Breakfast at Tiffany's*. It wasn't exactly the high point of her career. The critics panned the musical and crucified Mary. Little wonder that she ran right back to the safety of Pollyanna roles. But in August of 1966, when Mary finished filming *Millie* and began packing to move to

New York, she had no idea that she was heading into the worst disaster of her entire career.

Breakfast at Tiffany's—taken from the highly acclaimed novella by Truman Capote—had been successfully translated to the screen in 1961 with Audrey Hepburn and George Peppard in the leading roles. "Moon River"—the movie's haunting theme song—won an Oscar for composers Henry Mancini and Johnny Mercer and became one of Andy Williams's biggest record hits. Audrey Hepburn received a nomination, too, for her performance as the delightfully cynical, self-serving Holly Golightly. Later, when *Breakfast at Tiffany's*, the musical, was in its pre-Broadway death throes, the memory of both Miss Hepburn and "Moon River" had a great deal to do with the show's fate.

At the outset, the musicalization of Holly seemed like an inspired idea. Everyone connected with the project was a Broadway success story. Producer David Merrick was the man behind *Hello, Dolly!* and a long list of other superhits; Abe Burrows, the director-librettist, had been responsible for *Guys and Dolls*; and songwriter Bob Merrill had composed the scores for *Carnival* and *New Girl in Town*. As for the leads, everyone on Shubert Alley had his formula for the perfect showstopping combination. Some insiders were betting on Gwen Verdon and Richard Kiley, who'd been dynamite together in *Redhead* a few seasons back. Others had heard that the frontrunners for Holly Golightly were Tammy Grimes and Michele Lee—and insisted that *Carnival*'s Jerry Orbach had the inside track for the role of Holly's leading man.

David Merrick, however, had a far more dazzling brainstorm. He decided to team Richard Chamberlain and Mary Tyler Moore—Dr. Kildare and Laura Petrie—even though they had practically no live stage experience between them.

It was a new and totally unheard-of kind of theater producing—this concept of "fighting fire with fire." Merrick's thinking was very logical. If television was cutting into Broadway ticket sales, well, here was the perfect way to lure TV watchers back to the theater—by giving them a glimpse of TV's hottest young stars in the flesh (something that the boob tube, for all its right-in-your-living-room intimacy, couldn't provide).

Mary went into rehearsal for *Holly Golightly* (that's what the show was first called) in September 1966, a month after the wrap of *Thoroughly Modern Millie*. At that point, Merrick couldn't praise his young leading lady enough. At times he sounded more like her godfather or fan-club president than her producer. He hailed Mary as the next Mary Martin of the musical world. By the end of the production, he was calling her other—less flattering—names.

If Merrick's motives for hiring her were slightly gimmicky, Mary's motives for accepting were also somewhat complicated. True, the idea of starring on Broadway was irresistible, but Mary might never have said yes if geography hadn't worked in Merrick's favor. Grant Tinker, now a rising West Coast executive at NBC, had just been offered a promotion, but the promotion meant a transfer to the network's Rockefeller Center headquarters in Manhattan. If Mary did *Holly Golightly*, she could come east with Grant instead of forcing her husband to turn down the promotion (not likely) or forcing herself to accept a long-distance marriage (more likely).

From the start, Mary was nervous about singing and worried that her dance training wouldn't be enough to carry her through onstage. Before coming to New York she worked with a well-known voice coach, who put her in touch with a friend of his, a young Broadway musical actor. He took her in tow the minute she arrived in town.

"It was kind of an emergency situation," he remembered. "She was going into rehearsal very soon and she wasn't really ready. For my part, I was a little flabbergasted by the whole thing. I couldn't believe that Mary Tyler Moore was coming to me for advice. To begin with, I'd had no idea I'd be coaching her. One night I'd gotten a call from our mutual friend in Los Angeles and he said he'd been working with this young actress who really needed help. She was coming to New York to do a show—he'd done a crash program with her and frankly he hadn't had much luck. She was struggling and she was a nervous wreck. The upshot was that he asked me if I'd meet her when she got to New York, reassure her a little, maybe suggest the right voice teacher for her. I had the feeling she was really in trouble.

"He said, 'Let me give you her name and the telephone number where she'll be staying in New York—it's Mary Tyler Moore and she's coming in to do *Breakfast at Tiffany's*.' Well, I was absolutely floored. Up until he mentioned her name, I figured this was some little nobody, some girl off the street who'd gotten a small role in a show and was panicking over it. Mary Tyler Moore? I couldn't believe it.

"So I called her and we made contact. We went to a rehearsal studio and I listened to her sing. I don't remember what she sang exactly, but she was very nervous about it. That struck me as odd. If she was intimidated in that little room without an audience, how the hell was she going to survive onstage? After she sang, we chatted for a while —she was very nice, but scared. It was obvious she felt she was getting into a world about which she knew little. She was very eager to learn—she really wanted to do well—but she was so unsure of herself musically. I think, given more time and less pressure, she really would have succeeded, because underneath it all she really had singing talent. But at that point she just didn't know what she was doing with her voice. I gave her the names of four or five teachers who I thought could help her, but I don't know if she ever followed any of it up."

Mary later told reporter Phyllis Battelle that she should have been more skeptical about the project to start with. "I was nervous about the show, of course," she said, "but it was a healthy kind of nervousness. I should have been more nervous when I signed, because there wasn't even a second act. But it looked like it had to be the greatest hit in Broadway history. David Merrick, Abe Burrows directing, Michael Kidd for dances, Bob Merrill's songs, good story, even the Mark Hellinger Theatre [where *My Fair Lady* had opened]. Everything just spelled success. . . . But apparently it was a doomed project even before I went into it."

Was Mary right? Maybe her vocal problems were only a small part of the ills that plagued *Breakfast at Tiffany's*. The real culprit may have been the subject matter itself: Holly Golightly just wasn't the kind of heroine musical comedy audiences wanted to see. According to *Time*, all the out-of-town attempts to make Holly more appealing simply backfired. She went from being "a sweet fifty-dollar-a-shot hooker" to a "tough fifty-dollar-a-shot hooker" to a promiscuous dimwit "who might just shack up with anybody for nothing."

Those weren't the only strikes against Mary. In Philadelphia, Boston, and New York—the three cities where *Breakfast at Tiffany's* played—Mary was constantly being compared to Audrey Hepburn. People would wait for her at the stage door and tell her how disappointed they were that "Moon River" wasn't in the show—and David Merrick's high-powered publicity build-up only exacerbated the situation. How could anyone possibly live up to his inflated judgments of her musical capabilities? Merrick was constantly fueling Mary's insecurities with statements to the press like, "Who do we have in musical comedy anyhow? Barbara Harris can't sing and Barbra Streisand you can't get. Mary Tyler Moore has all the ingredients to be our next big musical comedy star."

Mary's doubts began to surface, though, right from the start. During the first run-through in New York, she made a slip of the tongue that stopped the entire cast in their tracks. Mary was supposed to say, "I'm going back to Brazil." The line came out, "I'm going back to California"—and for a second or two Mary didn't even realize what she'd said. They had to stop the run-through and tell her.

If that faux pas seemed a little on the Freudian side, so were some of the dreams Mary began having soon after moving to New York. She told *Saturday Evening Post* writer John Bowers about a few of them. In one, Mary dreamed that she was in an airplane crash and wound up stranded on a desert island. In another nightmare, recalling both her *Dick Van Dyke* and Hotpoint Pixie days, Mary dreamed of watching Morey Amsterdam bubbling down the kitchen drain until all she could see was a huge eye disappearing into the sink.

Some of her anxieties stemmed from the cross-country move. In transplanting themselves to New York, Mary and Grant had traded their spacious, two-story colonial house in Encino, California, for a twelve-room apartment on Fifth Avenue that they sublet from former NBC president Robert Kintner. Mary had a hard time adjusting to the noise, grit, traffic, and general seediness of the city. She enrolled her son Richie, now ten, in Trinity School, an exclusive Manhattan private school, and worried about his adjustment to their new life-style. Richie missed their big backyard in California and complained that he couldn't wear sneakers and dungarees to school in New York. It wasn't easy making friends in Manhattan, either. Mary didn't feel comfortable letting Richie wander all over the city by himself, taking buses and subways to other children's houses. Playing in the street was out of the question, too. Fifth Avenue was hardly designed for touch football.

Even the family dogs had a hard time adjusting. The Tinkers' German shepherd and miniature poodle had to go to obedience school to learn how to walk on a leash. A twelve-room apartment was certainly spacious by New York standards, but hardly enough romping room for two rambunctious pets who'd been allowed the run of the property back in California.

Mary worried about her son, her husband, the dogs, her singing, and particularly about crime. When Grant told her that one of his colleagues at NBC got mugged one night (it happened at 125th Street in Harlem—he was waiting to catch a commuter train to the suburbs there), Mary couldn't get the incident out of her mind. "I hope I don't wind up with an icepick in my heart," she joked to interviewers, trying to make light of her own feelings of uneasiness.

Going to work was hardly an antidote to her anxieties. *Breakfast at Tiffany's* became an increasingly terrifying experience for her. Mary suffered through each rehearsal with a bad case of sweaty palms and, before long, her knees were literally shaking onstage. At the same time, her co-star Richard Chamberlain came down with a bad cold. Mary's queasiness and Richard's sneeziness could have been taken as warning signals, which both Merrick and his associates chose to ignore. They were sure they had a major hit on their hands. Word of mouth was ringing up ticket sales like crazy. In Philadelphia and Boston, the box offices were completely sold out before the show ever left New

York. The Broadway advance sale was even more stagger-
ing, and had already passed the one-million-dollar mark.

Holly Golightly sailed into Philadelphia's Forrest Theatre
for its eagerly awaited world debut, and eventually limped
out of the City of Brotherly Love like a heavyweight contender who'd just been kayoed. During the first dress rehearsal Mary was starting to show signs of laryngitis, but
nobody panicked. Everyone, including Mary herself, as-
cribed it to pre–opening night jitters, or maybe a cold. That
afternoon another medical emergency took precedence
anyway: the actor who played the bartender in the show
got his hand caught in a piece of moving scenery and had
to be stitched up.

On opening night, however, Mary was a wreck, and a
doctor was called in to examine her. She was barely able to
speak, running a fever of 103°, and suffering from a bronchial infection which, months later, Mary told the press
had been "pneumonia." It seems odd, considering a diagno-
sis as serious as that, that David Merrick insisted on Mary
going on that night as scheduled—and that she agreed to it.

The doctors prescribed special medication to soothe her
throat. Julie Andrews, on hearing of Mary's illness, had a
silver box sent from Tiffany's, filled with throat lozenges
of the type that had helped Julie through her Broadway
runs of *My Fair Lady* and *Camelot.* The lozenges were made
especially for singers, but neither Julie's "medicine," nor
the doctor's, helped.

Mary whispered her way through the Philadelphia opening, displaying a range of approximately three notes. The
audience's reaction was devastating, but Mary was probably too sick and too medicated to be entirely aware of it. At
one point in the play, Holly stood outside her front door
and fumbled with her purse. "I've lost my goddam key,"
Mary croaked. "You sure have," someone in the audience

shouted. "Maybe you should take some singing lessons."

The Philadelphia critics not only found fault with Mary's performance, they had little regard for the entire production. They complained that Holly, whom Audrey Hepburn had played as such an endearing waif, had turned into a hard-nosed hooker in the musical. According to Harvey Sabinson, who handled the public relations on this ill-fated project, "The consensus among the Philadelphia critics was that it didn't measure up to the movie, and that there wasn't a song in it comparable to Johnny Mercer's 'Moon River.' "

Keeping her throat laced with honey, Mary somehow made it through the rest of the Philadelphia run, but new perils awaited the cast in Boston. During this time Merrick switched the show's title from *Holly Golightly* to *Breakfast at Tiffany's*, but that didn't stick either. He now kept changing the title back and forth so often that it became nearly impossible to print up programs for the show or run advertisements.

The title confusion was just a small reflection of the backstage pandemonium that broke out. When the Boston reviews proved even worse than the Philadelphia pans (the *Boston Globe* called *Breakfast at Tiffany's* "a straightforward musical flop"), Merrick decided to take drastic action. He hired playwright Edward Albee to rewrite the libretto which Abe Burrows and his partner, Nunnally Johnson, had created. Albee seemed a strange choice indeed as script surgeon for an ailing musical. Most Broadway producers would have called in Comden and Green or Neil Simon— someone to tighten the dialogue and punch up the jokes. Albee had never written a musical in his life, and as a dramatist was mainly known for delineating neurotic decadence in such plays as *Who's Afraid of Virginia Woolf?* and *Tiny Alice*. How in the world could he put the spark—not to mention sparkle—back into a project like this? It didn't seem feasible. But Merrick believed that Albee might actually be able to produce a script that was closer to Truman Capote's original novella than either the movie version or the Johnson-Burrows adaptation had been. It was an adventurous risk, certainly, but considering the fact that $500,000 had already been spent on *Breakfast at Tiffany's*, perhaps the time had come for an extreme measure.

Merrick managed to convince Abe Burrows to stay on as director while stepping down as librettist. Now the fun begins. During the day the cast would rehearse the new version (by Albee) while continuing to play the old version (by Johnson-Burrows) at night. Since there were substantial differences in the tone of the two scripts—and significant character changes—it took nerves of steel to get through those horrifying weeks in Boston. As the leads, Mary and Richard Chamberlain were handed the most changes—and for their trouble took the most flak.

The honeymoon between Abe Burrows and Edward Albee was over in record time. Burrows walked, and was replaced by director Joseph Anthony. In his autobiography, *Is There Really No Business Like Show Business?*, Abe Burrows defends his libretto against Albee's, remarking that "it was a financial success out of town. The reviews were somewhat mixed but the houses were always full and the people in the audience seemed to enjoy themselves." He then adds that he couldn't sanction Albee's "approach" to the show: "His ideas called for what was practically a whole new show, and I didn't want to direct it."

The Albee version didn't actually play in front of a live audience until the show returned to New York and began previews. But first Mary and the rest of the cast had to make it through Boston. On December 1, 1966—just as the show was folding in Boston for its return trip to New York —the *New York Post* printed an exclusive interview that

Mary had granted columnist Sheilah Graham. "I'll be afraid to go into Sardi's. Everyone will be looking at me and saying 'Poor girl.' . . . I've got to clear my name. It's been the roughest time of my life." She said that the month-long engagement in Boston seemed like fourteen. "You can imagine how I felt having to go on every night when I read that Tammy Grimes or Diahann Carroll would replace me."

In Philadelphia the critics had panned Mary for playing Holly as tough and cynical; in Boston the script had gone to the other extreme and turned Holly into a sexual sister of charity. Mary was trounced for that too. But nobody, including Mary, was quite prepared for the Edward Albee concept of Holly Golightly that emerged during the first New York preview. Mary herself called that last incarnation of Holly "fascinating," but it was truly a 180-degree turn from her all-American image. Mary was now playing a cheap tart who, in typical Albee fashion, was far more appalling than appealing. And if Holly wasn't exactly a musical heroine in the grand tradition of Mame or Dolly, well, the show was no longer much of a musical anyway. Albee had deleted so many songs the week before New York previews began that *Breakfast at Tiffany's* was now being promoted as "a play with music." Theatergoers didn't know whether they were watching a comedy, a tragedy, or a satire of the whole musical-comedy art form.

If Merrick was afraid that New York audiences would kill the show, it was perhaps his best hunch to date. During the first preview, the audience laughed at the play's most serious moments and occasionally ad-libbed their own responses to the dialogue. When Holly announced that she needed to find a doctor for an abortion, someone in the back of the theater stood up and yelled, "Go see a lawyer instead and get yourself out of this show!"

By that time, baiting the cast had become half the reason

for buying a preview ticket—and New Yorkers flocked to see *Breakfast at Tiffany's* with the same rowdiness usually reserved for Mets games. Whatever affection lay behind those Bronx cheers was lost on Mary. "They'd told me that preview audiences are rude," she said. "But I don't think anybody ever played to the kind of rudeness we put up with. It was humiliating." The raucous laughter at all the wrong moments hurt the most. Mary called it "the most crushing blow an actor ever has to endure—I don't think I could face it again."

By the second preview, only a portion of the audience actually sat through the entire performance. The third preview was even more disastrous, and David Merrick, calling *Breakfast at Tiffany's* his "Bay of Pigs," decided to close the show without ever subjecting it to an official Broadway opening. Once the huge advance sale was refunded, the show was $400,000 in the red, and Merrick, the largest investor, suffered the biggest financial loss.

For Mary Tyler Moore and Richard Chamberlain, the losses were the kind that can't be measured in, or compensated by, money. The emotional blows were far more devastating. Neither of them held a grudge against David Merrick, and they took turns assuring the press that "closing the show had been the only sensible decision." Mary felt her singing had improved substantially since Philadelphia, and she was glad the public had a chance to know that. She had no hard feelings, no regrets. It was like putting a sick animal out of its misery—it's tragic, but what can you do?

David Merrick—now a few hundred thousand dollars lighter—never lost his sense of humor. He announced that only one organization, Cartier's, had begged him to keep the show open. They were sure it would permanently ruin the reputation of Tiffany's.

After the final performance, Mary held a wake for the

whole cast at Sardi's. Then she went home with her husband to cry in private.

Richard Chamberlain wept, too. As he later confided to
Rex Reed, "I got very manic and uptight. I walked past the
marquee to see my name in lights for one last time, and
then I cried all night." After that, Chamberlain spent four
years in analysis.

Mary Tyler Moore had arrived in New York telling reporters, "I'm doing this show for only one person—*me*. I
have to prove to myself that I can do it. I have to be the
best." Later, long after Mary was back in California making another movie for Universal, Shubert Alley was still
full of Monday morning quarterbacks who knew just what
was wrong with *Breakfast at Tiffany's* and were only too
eager to share their better-late-than-never flashes of wisdom:

"If only Merrick had delayed the opening a few weeks
longer . . ."

"If only they'd kept Abe Burrows's libretto—that's
where the laughs were . . ."

"If only they'd opened at a smaller theater—that kind of
show needed an intimate feeling . . ."

But Mary, the perfectionist, felt the truth lay a little
closer to home. In March 1967—sitting in the Universal
commissary with reporter Phyllis Battelle, feeling safe and
secure again—Mary did something a star almost never
does. She took the blame. "You know," she said, "I've seen
some shows come to Broadway that were not so great. Like
The Apple Tree and *Funny Girl*. But the stars [Barbara Harris, Barbra Streisand] pulled them through. And I've felt it
maybe was my fault that my show didn't survive . . ."

✤ 4 ✤

Choices

Breakfast at Tiffany's had robbed Mary of her professional dignity—stripped her down to bare bones in public—and it took her a long time to get over that. During the show's run, and for nearly a year afterward, she had recurring nightmares about drowning. In her dreams, she was stranded on a beach—all alone—and huge tidal waves were engulfing her. "I fight, but they carry me away," she told reporter John Bowers. "I claw at the sand, and yet they take me away. I don't know why I dream it. I love the sea."

In a way, New York—that vast ocean of grime and concrete, not to mention endless waves of humanity (and inhumanity)—had hit her with hurricane force. After years of quiet California living, Mary found it difficult to readjust. She longed for home. She tried to involve herself in things, but nothing filled the void. She enrolled in ballet class, shopped to her heart's content from Greenwich Village to Fifty-seventh Street, and lunched at all the smart places. She even got together with Richard Chamberlain now and then for old time's sake. "We took Richie to Radio City and reminisced about Breakfast at Tiffany's," she said. "It was either a sign that we were both very healthy or very masochistic."

Mary knew she was just passing the time and so did her

husband Grant. In fact, he was so worried about her that
he rearranged his own work situation so they could get
back to California quickly. Right after the first of the year,
Grant left NBC and accepted an offer from Mary's home
studio, Universal, to become a vice president. It was their
ticket back to Los Angeles. "You mean I won't have to wait
for an elevator every time I want to walk the dogs?" Mary
joked when he broke the news to her. On the day they left
for the airport, Mary was so elated she even waved goodbye to the bums in Central Park as their taxi sped cross-
town.

In March 1967—just three months after David Merrick
had signed her Broadway death certificate—Mary was back
in Los Angeles and starting to revive again. The Tinkers
were once more ensconced in a house with a swimming
pool and patio (they were renting Dinah Shore and George
Montgomery's old digs) and tanning themselves to an ap-
propriate shade of bronze while waiting for *Thoroughly
Modern Millie* to open. Mary felt ready to make pictures
again and was anxious to fulfill the rest of her Universal
contract. She still scoffed at the thought of ever returning
to television. That kind of stardom was okay, she said—"it's
nice to be able to open a charge account anywhere, no
questions asked"—but walking into the commissary at
Universal and seeing her photo on the same wall with Julie
Andrews and Doris Day and Elvis Presley—that was the
real high! It put a lot of confidence back in her step.

Mary, however, was so eager to be a motion-picture star
that she gave Universal carte blanche control of her des-
tiny. Unfortunately, they chose scripts for her the same
way Othello handled his love life—not wisely, but too well.
"They just threw me into whatever movies came along,"
Mary later said. It's a wonder they didn't try to stick her
on a motorcycle and team her with Hell's Angels. But who

knows? Even that might have been an improvement over some of the second-rate pap that Mary waded through trying to become a recycled Doris Day.

In *Don't Just Stand There!* (released in May 1968), Mary was out to save a female sex novelist from a band of smugglers. As a reward for her troubles, Mary sailed off into the Aegean sunset with Robert Wagner in the last frame—but practically all the other frames belonged to Glynis Johns, who stole what little of the script there was to steal as the pornographic pen pusher. Needless to say, the film didn't draw crowds away from Barbra Streisand's *Funny Girl* or Mel Brooks's *The Producers*, both of which also came out in the summer of 1968.

That same summer Mary was also on display in *What's So Bad about Feeling Good?*, another film that didn't light any box-office fires. This time Mary and her leading man, George Peppard, were slightly over-the-hill hippies padding through Greenwich Village in their beads and sandals. The real star of the film, though, was Amigo, a tropical bird that infected people with instant happiness. Actually, Mary was the only person in the film who never caught the virus, but perhaps we should all be grateful for small favors. Mary's character was so sweet to begin with that if the bird had infected her, he probably would have killed her with kindness.

Mary's film ventures were pretty laughable—except that audiences weren't laughing with her, at least not in droves —and in 1968 Mary began to think seriously about retiring from show business. Since leaving *The Dick Van Dyke Show* nothing had really worked out for her. She had failed on Broadway—and so far her film career wasn't a dazzling success. It seemed like a good time to tread water for a while and catch up on other areas of her life. Richie was twelve years old, practically a teenager. Mary had never

thought much about whether she wanted another child—
she was always too busy working—but now, at the age of
thirty, not really knowing what to do next with her life,
Mary decided to become pregnant.

Her anticipation was short-lived. The pregnancy ended
in miscarriage; and within hours a routine blood test in the
hospital revealed that Mary was suffering from diabetes.
She couldn't cope with the news. She was still struggling
to come to terms with the loss of her baby—how could she
possibly be expected to deal with this other "sickness," as
she described it? Mary knew very little about the disease,
but decided that in her case there must be some mistake.
She thought of diabetics as invalids and had vague notions
of them leading a fragile, shut-in existence. That certainly
wasn't her. As soon as she could get up and around, and
leave the damn hospital, she knew she'd be fine again.

What Mary needed most was a positive attitude. Knowing it could make the crucial difference between success
and failure in her treatment, her doctor tried to gently ease
her into accepting her condition. He put her on a relatively
mild program of treatment. No insulin—just the drug Ori-
nase, which she could take orally. Her diet was restricted
—sweets were out, so was liquor—but all in all Mary's life
wasn't being tampered with too much at that point. Maybe
that's why she refused to take her condition seriously.
More likely, after all the emotional battering she'd been
through in the last two years, Mary simply didn't care.

She reacted with almost total denial—indulging in the
kind of self-destructive behavior that had never been her
style. Her diet went out the window. She started bringing
gooey desserts into the house. When Grant tried to stop
her, she began sneak-eating on the sly—cookies, cake, all
her favorite forbidden foods. "I'd sit in my car in the supermarket parking lot munching everything I wasn't sup-

posed to," Mary remembers. "I became more and more cavalier about my diet, and I wasn't getting enough exercise or nearly enough rest. I fooled myself into believing that my doctors were worrywarts."

But the state of collapse that occurred turned out to be alarmingly real, and Mary had to be admitted to the hospital again. Her condition had worsened so much that, from now on, she would need injections of insulin twice a day, for the rest of her life.

At first, Mary refused to learn how to treat herself. She insisted that someone else give her the hypodermic injections each day. But that meant constant trips to the doctor's office. Finally, practicality won out, and Mary began to learn how to give herself insulin. She also began seeing a psychoanalyst, who helped her deal with her illness and tried to get her back on the right track emotionally.

In analysis, she became an educated diabetic and learned that if she could maintain the right balance between diet, exercise, and her insulin intake, she could lead an active, healthy life. The trick was to control the disease, not let the disease control her. Mary, the defiant one, blossomed into a model patient. She started thinking of diabetes as a "malfunction," not an illness. "Medication keeps it in control," she said. "I give myself injections morning and night. I don't have any strict diet. I dance and exercise every day and I don't run down. . . . In fact, I'm as strong and healthy as a horse."

Occasionally, she'd still binge and eat six doughnuts in a row—"maybe it's part of thumbing my nose at doctors and at fate," she admitted—but her main indulgences were diet cola and cigarettes. She still had mixed feelings, though, about discussing her health in public. Undoubtedly, the fact that Mary Tyler Moore had diabetes—and was controlling it—could be a source of inspiration to other diabetics, but Mary sometimes felt her personal story was being turned into a true-confession saga by the press. "Some of the fan magazines made it such a big deal," she told reporter Hank McCann. "It became a circus of stories about Mary Tyler Moore's disease and hints about how I was at the end of the line. Eecchh!"

Once Mary got a handle on her health, she dropped her analyst. He was a Freudian; she spent every session on the couch, which made her feel uncomfortable and inhibited. "He only asked questions, he never really spoke," Mary said, "and I couldn't think of anything very enlightening to say. Our sessions were like scenes from some theater-of-the-absurd play. There was no communication at all. So, finally, I quit. Even that didn't get a rise out of him."

Mary left analysis with the question that had brought her into therapy unanswered: What am I going to do with my life? "I wasn't a hostess or a terrific gardener or a great cook," she later said. "My son was practically grown up and I knew I wouldn't be having any more babies. So what could I do with myself? Did I want to be an actress again? I wasn't sure. I had my needlepoint and my crossword puzzles—it was hardly what you'd call a career."

Eventually, Mary ran out of needlepoint patterns—and it was too early to wrap next year's Christmas presents—so she agreed to do another film for Universal. This project was *Change of Habit*, and Mary was cast in her most socially significant role to date. She played Sister Michelle, a modern nun who was tempted to try first a home permanent, then skirts above the knee, and finally a little romance with a sexy young doctor. The dedicated medic (who ran a free clinic in the barrio) was played by Elvis Presley, and obviously all the vows of chastity in the world were no match for him. While Mary kept lighting candles, Elvis kept lighting fires of a different kind, and by the end of the film her Mother Superior was forcing her to make a drastic choice: Mary could have Elvis or the Church—not both. Practically every American woman under forty, who'd been raised on *Love Me Tender* and *Blue Hawaii*, had a hard time understanding what the fuss was all about—and that was only one of the film's problems. One critic caustically referred to it as "*The Sound of Music* goes slumming"; and both the film and Mary's performance in it were quickly forgotten. There was only one fringe benefit for Mary: on the set she met Edward Asner, who had a small role as a police lieutenant.

Once again Mary had to move on—but where? As *TV Guide*'s Dwight Whitney explained, in the years since the demise of *The Dick Van Dyke Show*, Mary had earned the title of "America's Pluckiest Loser." The public applauded her zeal and perseverance in spite of one failure after another, but sympathy and pity didn't translate into exciting film and TV offers. Even if Mary now wanted to return to television, the doors might not be open to her. "The industry now found it all too easy to believe," wrote Whitney, "that Mary wasn't really all that zingy but had merely ridden to her Emmys on the coattails of Van Dyke."

Ironically, it was Van Dyke who came to her rescue now. In the spring of 1969—just after she had finished filming *Change of Habit*—he approached her with the idea of the two of them doing a "reunion" special for CBS. Mary eagerly accepted. The show was a happy blend of comedy, music, and nostalgia—Mary and Dick played a bride and groom on top of a four-tiered wedding cake, they sang, they danced, they reminisced about their days as Rob and Laura Petrie—and the ratings went through the roof. The special was a Nielsen top-ten winner for the week and much higher rated than Dick's previous variety special with Leslie Uggams. It made CBS think twice about Mary. Maybe she had more drawing power than they realized.

The network offered her a deal to do "anything she wanted," and Mary set her sights on a new comedy series. Grant, who was now a vice president at 20th Century–Fox, and her business manager, Arthur Price, worked out a multimillion-dollar agreement with CBS, which gave Mary a substantial amount of creative clout as well as ownership rights to her new show. If her series became a hit and was eventually sold into reruns (where the real profits are in TV), Mary might conceivably end up like Lucille Ball—richer than most movie stars. Mary signed the deal in September 1969—just two months before the release of *Change of Habit*—and shelved the rest of her contract with Universal.

Now all she had to do was come up with a format for *The Mary Tyler Moore Show*. Grant set up MTM Enterprises and hired two writers, James L. Brooks and Allan Burns, who'd collaborated on *Room 222* for 20th Century–Fox TV. They started brainstorming immediately: Mary would be dating two guys at the same time. No, too cute. Mary would be a gal Friday for a gossip columnist. No, too dumb. Mary would be a nun working with a hippie priest—after *Change of Habit*, Heaven forbid!

Mary herself had only one stipulation—no more suburban homemaker scenarios. "I didn't want to do another husband-and-wife show because I was afraid it would be unfavorably compared with the *Dick Van Dyke* series," she said. CBS thought she might make a great widow with three kids. After all, Doris Day had two orphaned boys on her show and Diahann Carroll (*Julia*) was raising a fatherless son, too. "I guess they figured I'd be an even bigger hit with one extra child," Mary laughed.

She ruled out children, widowhood, roommates, a dog, even a steady boyfriend—all the traditional accessories for helpless situation-comedy heroines. What Mary wanted to play was a divorcée—and that had never been done before. When Jim Brooks and Allan Burns brought that idea to a summit meeting of CBS executives, they weren't exactly welcomed with open arms. Later, in a *New York Times Magazine* interview with Tracy Johnston, Burns recalled how the network reacted to the mere mention of the word *divorce:* "We sat there in a room full of divorced New York Jews with mustaches and heard them say that there are four things Americans don't like: New Yorkers, divorced people, men with mustaches, and Jews. It was strongly hinted that if we insisted on having Mary divorced, the show would go on at one in the morning."

Instead, Mary Richards became a single girl, but she was over thirty and she had a past. In the first script, Mary briefly reviewed her life before coming to Minneapolis: she had helped put her boyfriend through medical school—it wasn't specifically mentioned but they had probably lived together—and then the fink wouldn't marry her. Not exactly the sort of admission you'd expect from Marlo Thomas or Sally Field.

The show was set in 1970, and focused on Mary's new life in Minneapolis. Working at WJM as assistant producer of *The Six o'Clock News,* she was surrounded by an assortment of lovable oddballs: Ted Baxter, the dumb anchorman; Murray Slaughter, the self-deprecating news writer; and Lou Grant, the hard-boiled producer. At home, in her cozy studio apartment with the ruffled curtains, claustrophobic kitchenette, and sofa bed in the living room—a typical single girl's Shangri-la—Mary coped with her neighbors. There was Phyllis Lindstrom, her neurotic landlady, and Rhoda Morgenstern, her brash new friend from the Bronx.

Rhoda dropped by constantly to raid Mary's refrigerator and hash over their latest problems, which usually involved men, waistlines, and work. Actually, Mary was the first situation-comedy heroine to work at a real job. Most of her predecessors on the sitcom scene looked like they'd never dare do anything that might endanger their freshly manicured fingernails—unless you count Sally Field's excursions on *The Flying Nun* as part-time aviation. On *That Girl*, Marlo Thomas only pursued acting jobs in between dates with Ted Bessell, and the daughters on *Petticoat Junction* barely helped with the dishes. Mary made nine-to-fivers respectable. Her job wasn't really glamorous; it was mainly uneventful. In creating WJM, Jim Brooks and Allan Burns had visited local TV and radio news stations all over Los Angeles to get a realistic handle on the setting and characters. "In every one, we found a Ted, a Lou, and a Murray," they later revealed. (Later on, Walter Cronkite told them that WJM reminded him very much of a newsroom he had worked in during his early days as a reporter.)

All through the spring and summer of 1970, the MTM creative team struggled to put a show together that would be funny, sophisticated, and at the same time middle-of-the-road enough to pass muster at CBS. Meanwhile, Mary and Grant tried not to hover over everyone's shoulder like expectant parents. The Tinkers stayed close to their sprawling house on Beverly Drive (in the most elegant part of Beverly Hills) and waited for the first scripts to come in. They continued to live in only semi-splendor, California style. Richie, now fourteen, was spending a good deal of time with his father in Fresno; the house was empty except for Grant and Mary's three dogs—Maud, Diswilliam, and Maxim de Winter (whom Mary had named after the Laurence Olivier character in *Rebecca*). Grant drove a Cadillac,

Mary had an XKE, but she maintained that they were basically "barefoot people," who liked nothing better than to loll around the patio in their sweatshirts and Levis. Barbecuing—like tennis and needlepoint—was still the backbone of Mary's private existence.

But as fall drew closer, Mary couldn't keep her mind on the back-yard grill. She was too busy worrying about the royal roasting that her new comedy show might get. The early signs didn't look good. According to word of mouth, *The Mary Tyler Moore Show* was too sophisticated to play in Peoria—or practically anywhere else in Middle America. Herb Jacobs—a powerful TV prognosticator—loudly predicted that Mary's show would be the first new series canceled in the 1970–71 season. Jim Brooks and Allan Burns held a press conference for TV editors and columnists and tried to explain what *The Mary Tyler Moore Show* was all about. They didn't convince anyone, except maybe a few busboys who served the lunch. TV columnist Hank McCann remembers the occasion very well. "At the conclusion of the conference—a somewhat disjointed hour of long pauses and barbed questions," he wrote, "the consensus was that Mary Tyler Moore was headed toward disaster. She and her producers didn't seem to know where they were going or what they were trying to accomplish with their story."

For better or worse, the cast moved into the CBS Studio Center on Radford Avenue in North Hollywood. Mary's dressing-room trailer—beautifully decorated in yellow and green—consisted of a kitchen, bedroom, and living room. Someone joked that it was bigger than Mary Richards's apartment on the show. The trailer was also located right onstage, so that Mary could be out of her "home away from home" and on the set in ten seconds flat.

The first preview before a live audience was a disaster. Mary didn't think the show was all that funny; the audience reaction was lukewarm. She feared that she might have gotten trapped into another *Holly Golightly*—and demanded changes. The writers, realizing that the show still had many kinks to iron out, stayed up all night trying to accommodate Mary's revisions and their own.

Mary felt ill-at-ease in the newsroom, but that turned out to be a plus for the show. After all, Mary Richards was supposed to be a newcomer—it was her first day on the job —and so it was perfectly natural for her to be a bit overwhelmed by it all. But Mary's other complaint was harder to remedy. She didn't like, or understand, the character of Rhoda Morgenstern. Word had already leaked out that Rhoda's character was funnier than Mary's and—according to one TV critic—"Valerie Harper was threatening to steal the show." Burns and Brooks solved that problem by incorporating Mary's wariness right into the script. Her first reaction to meeting Rhoda was genuine dislike. Mary thought Rhoda was too aggressive and too cynical. Rhoda took one look at her new neighbor and resented the fact that anyone could be so perfect—and so thin. Then, slowly but surely, as Mary and Valerie learned to put their guard down backstage, their on-screen friendship began to blossom in the script.

CBS put *The Mary Tyler Moore Show* in a Saturday-night time slot, sandwiched between another new comedy series, *Arnie,* and a veteran ratings-getter, *Mannix.* To everyone's surprise—despite all the predictions to the contrary— Mary's premiere episode on September 19, 1970, did reasonably well, and the show kept gathering momentum from that point on. In fact, it caught on far more quickly than *The Dick Van Dyke Show* had. All through its first season, *MTM* made a fairly respectable showing in the ratings and finished in twenty-second place—just a decimal point ahead of NBC's *Saturday Night Movie.* Mary managed to demolish the ABC entry—*The Most Deadly Game,* a detective series with George Maharis—in less than four months.

MTM, The Flip Wilson Show, and *All in the Family* turned out to be the most talked about (and most watched) new hits of 1970–71.

Everyone had a reason why *The Mary Tyler Moore Show* succeeded. Harry Ackerman—the man who helped create *Bewitched*—thought there was a nonthreatening likability factor involved, a quality that Mary shared with Elizabeth Montgomery. "They both exude a wholesome sex appeal," he said. "Women don't resent them and men can have their daydreams." Jim Brooks had another theory—Spiro Agnew. Agnew's constant battles with the press had made the country news-conscious—people liked the fact that *Mary Tyler Moore* took you behind the scenes and showed how a newsroom really functioned. (As the years went on, Brooks's theory became even more valid; *MTM* reached its zenith in the ratings during the Watergate era, when the *Washington Post*'s Woodward and Bernstein became national heroes and America idolized the press.)

Mary herself had another theory about her success. She realized that, aside from Lucille Ball and Carol Burnett, very few women had ever become long-running television clowns. "The public has trouble accepting women as both funny and feminine," Mary declared. "On my show I'm surrounded by Ed Asner, Ted Knight, and Gavin MacLeod. They get the laughs and I get the straight lines, so I suppose the public doesn't think of me as such a funny lady."

Some memorable things happened during that first season. Rhoda's cranky mother, Ida Morgenstern, played by Nancy Walker, paid a surprise visit from the Bronx and, like the man who came to dinner, meddled incessantly. Mary went out with "Eric the Shrimp," a very embarrassing Romeo who had to stand on a telephone book to kiss her good night. And Mary gave the first in her long line of doomed parties. Later on in the series, Mary, the frazzled hostess, would battle blackouts and a shortage of veal Prince Orloff; this time Rhoda's escort was enough to cast an instant pall. She invited a man she had recently dented fenders with—and he brought along his wife.

On May 9, 1971, the Academy of Television Arts and Sciences bestowed its annual blessings on the industry—and as usual Emmy fever ran high. *The Mary Tyler Moore Show* was nominated in every comedy category (except best leading actor) and won four important prizes: best supporting actor and actress (Edward Asner and Valerie Harper), best writing (James Brooks and Allan Burns for the Ida Morgenstern episode, "Support Your Local Mother"), and best directing (Jay Sandrich for the "Eric the Shrimp" segment). Nevertheless, despite the *MTM* surge, *All in the Family* was voted outstanding comedy series of the year, and Jean Stapleton—not Mary—was named best actress.

A year later, the results were virtually the same. *All in the Family* and Jean Stapleton took top honors again and Ed Asner was named best supporting actor. Valerie Harper repeated her 1971 win, too, but this time she tied with *All in the Family*'s Sally Struthers.

In their acceptance speeches, Ed Asner and Valerie Harper kept remarking that part of their Emmies really belonged to Mary Tyler Moore—she was the glue that held the whole cast together—and the TV Academy finally rectified that oversight on May 22, 1973. That year Mary was named best actress in a comedy series—and it was Jean Stapleton, not Mary, who had to sit through the rest of the ceremonies trying her best not to look crestfallen. Valerie

Harper took home her third Emmy, and Ted Knight, who was named best supporting actor, became the fourth *MTM* cast member to join the TV Academy winners' circle.

Professionally, Mary was at the zenith. Her show finished in seventh place for the season; thirty million Americans stopped going out to dinner on Saturday night just to watch her; and even the *New Yorker*—a magazine that ranked television as only slightly less harmful than tetanus—acknowledged her presence by making a joke about "MTM watching" in one of its cartoons. Mary had become the golden girl of the Nielsens and the goddess of the sophisticates. The same New Yorkers who had once booed her on Broadway now worshipped at her CBS shrine. Daniel Menaker, writing in *The New York Times Magazine*, explained how Mary was affecting civilization on Manhattan's Upper East Side. "Mary is so In, actually," he wrote, "that it has become especially fashionable to drift into the den at a party—or even go home—at 9 on Saturday night because you 'simply must not miss' her program."

Only one person joked that he'd love to sabotage *The Mary Tyler Moore Show*—her old co-star Dick Van Dyke. And who could blame him? If Mary's comeback had failed, then she might have been available to reteam with him when he launched his own comedy venture, *The New Dick Van Dyke Show*, in 1971. Instead, he had to settle for Hope Lange as a replacement wife, and somehow their partnership never set off the same sweet and zany sparks that Dick and Mary had generated together. Maybe America had never really accepted the breakup. In the public's eyes, it was probably okay for Mary to be single. As long as she was without a man, it didn't threaten any of their prior fantasies. But it was not okay for Dick to have a new wife—that was a betrayal.

Dick Van Dyke knew all along that Mary Tyler Moore

was the best thing that had ever happened to him. Back in 1970, when she first returned to television, he had watched with mixed feelings as she sailed into Minneapolis—her chin up, choking back nervous tears but determined to make it on her own. Then he turned off the set and said with a mournful grin, "Gosh, I'd like to torpedo that show and get Mary back."

❧ 5 ❧

A Closed Corporation

While Dick Van Dyke was wrinkling his pajamas in the same TV bed as Hope Lange, Mary Richards continued to lead a more solitary existence. Most of her dates ended with a perfunctory kiss at the front door. Like many "New Women" of the 1970s, Mary wasn't exactly virginal—she enjoyed her share of sexual adventures now and then—but mainly she resisted getting involved. Being cast as Mary's new boyfriend was known as the *MTM* kiss of death. "Oh, you're playing Mary's new guy," a stagehand told one unsuspecting guest star. "Don't bother to get too comfortable —you won't be here long."

Another actor—who came out from New York to do the show—asked his agent whether he should check into a hotel room or start looking for a house. His agent immediately set him straight: "Listen, the only thing I'd look for is a cab—to get back to the airport."

Americans, it seemed, liked their favorite girl next door just the way she was—with her libido at a low agitation level—and Mary was happy to oblige. She actively discouraged the writers from building a permanent love interest for her because, frankly, she was enjoying her character's freedom too much to give it up. Independence was something the on-screen Mary had that the real Mary lacked. She had gone straight from high school into one marriage after another with barely a moment in between to catch her breath. "In some ways, I envy Mary Richards' situation," Mary Tyler Moore once said. "She has an interesting job, terrific friends, a very attractive life. She's independent, but rarely lonely."

The show's writers, who were poor matchmakers, kept trying to fix Mary up. Her early admirers included Michael Tolan (a suave journalism professor) and Richard Schaal (her bumbling hometown sweetheart). Later on, she inherited Ted Bessell—Marlo Thomas's old boyfriend—but that didn't work out, either.

John Gabriel, who played sportscaster Andy Rivers, gave Mary Richards her first on-camera kiss and managed to hang in for five episodes. He practically set a record, if not in the *Guinness Book of Records*, then at least in Mary's dating diary! The kiss itself was rehearsed as carefully as delicate surgery. It couldn't be too adolescent (Mary, after all, was past thirty) or too passionate (remember, some people still thought she was Mrs. Dick Van Dyke). In the end, John and Mary managed to strike just the right balance between fire and ice, although with so many producers, cameramen, and network people watching, it's amazing they were able to sustain a pucker at all. Somebody on the set joked, "The preparations for this moment have lasted longer than some marriages!"

Luckily, John Gabriel only had to expose his lips to the scrutiny of Mary Tyler Moore's fans. He didn't have to strip down to his underwear. That dubious honor belonged to another actor who made a flash (or should we say flasher?)-in-the-pan appearance during the show's last season. John Reilly, who had just spent three years playing a dedicated medic on *As the World Turns*, was cast as a swinging bachelor who'd obviously never read the book *Dress for*

Success. "I played the ultimate egotistical male," he recalls. "When Mary invited me in for a cup of coffee after a date, I immediately got the wrong idea and started taking my clothes off. Mary didn't even ask if I wanted cream or sugar —she just threw me out!"

Although John is a strapping six-foot Irishman, he started to get wobbly knees during rehearsal. TV studios (even in sunny California) are always on the drafty side; and for John it was more a case of chills than thrills, stepping in and out of his pants every time he did the scene. Once a shirt button popped; another time his zipper got stuck. The cameramen thought the whole thing was hilarious, and soon John and Mary were cracking up, too.

"I was a little intimidated the first time we rehearsed that scene," John admits, "but Mary was such a joy to work with that I relaxed into it very quickly. I think to a large extent that's why the show was so successful—because Mary never behaved like a *star* on the set. She always acted like a human being and treated everyone as her colleagues, not as underlings. Once, during a run-through, I went up on my lines. Instead of getting angry and stopping the scene, she began helping me out, incorporating my lines into her speech."

Mary's disastrous dates weren't the only spark of hilarity on the show. *MTM* poked gentle fun at a wide range of human foibles: Rhoda's weight problem, Murray's baldness, Ted's stupidity, and Sue Ann's nymphomania. The comedy was always sharp but never slapstick, and some of the show's best moments evoked, strangely enough, tears, not laughter. The breakup of Lou's marriage, Murray's sense of frustration as a failed writer, Rhoda's battles with her mother, and those painful flashes of the frightened little boy inside Ted Baxter—these weren't the kind of things you'd expect to see on *Three's Company*. Actually, *The Mary*

Tyler Moore Show wasn't a situation comedy at all—it was more a drama with laughter or, if you prefer, a comedy with tears. In one way or another, every character was a bit frayed around the edges. In fact, it was their imperfections, so like our own, that we laughed at—and loved.

Even Mary had her dark side, though it was several wholesome layers beneath the surface. As *Newsweek* remarked, "Mary can wrap an insult in velvet and put down a lover so gently that he never knows what happened until he wakes up on the sidewalk outside her apartment." In the show's opening episode, Lou Grant told Mary she definitely had *spunk*, then gruffly informed her, "I hate spunk." A few seasons later, Mary confided that she secretly hated it too. "Mr. Grant, you don't know what it's like being a perky, cute person," she sobbed. "No one realizes what's bubbling underneath: the doubts, fears, worries, tensions."

Unfortunately, that's exactly how Mary herself felt during her *MTM* years. On the set, she was cooperative, enthusiastic, far from a wave-maker—but she never really opened up to anyone either. When *Playboy* interviewer Sam Merrill asked Ed Asner, "What's Mary Tyler Moore really like?" Asner replied, "For seven years, she did great work and contributed to a happy set. But personally, Mary is a closed corporation."

In the early 1970s, heroes and heroines were in short supply—Vietnam and Watergate had destroyed too many national illusions—but no matter what your politics, Mary Tyler Moore was one woman everyone could admire. People knew very little about the actress herself. She rarely gave interviews and even then only on selected subjects, but in the public's mind, somehow the real Mary Tyler Moore and her on-screen counterpart had blended into one eternally happy Girl Scout. She could do no wrong. Everything that happened in her own life somehow enhanced her all-American image. Nothing—not even her separation from Grant Tinker in 1973—could detract from it.

Leave it to Mary Tyler Moore to have a "happy" marital split. The estrangement, which occurred just after Thanksgiving and lasted only six weeks, turned out to be—according to Mary—"one of the greatest learning experiences of my life. Grant and I were both working so hard that we weren't communicating as well as we should have been. We had stopped listening. We were building a beach house at the time. He thought I wanted it—I thought he did—it all got very mixed-up. Being apart was the best thing that could have happened to us, because we found out how much we wanted to be together. Now our relationship is stronger than it's ever been because we've learned how to listen to each other again."

Meanwhile, despite her marital ups and downs, Mary continued to function on a very even keel professionally. According to many critics, her portrayal of Mary Richards was the best work of her career and helped bring TV out of the dark ages of cornball comedy forever. Although Mary herself was nowhere near as funny as Ted or Rhoda or Lou, she was the hub character of the show—the sensible anchor in a sea of zanies. Her reactions made everything else *seem* funny. But unlike Lucy Ricardo (or even Laura Petrie), Mary never stooped to the level of the ridiculous. She didn't get zapped by exploding toasters or sabotaged by bathtub drains. She never had a single urge to dress up in a silly disguise or climb out on a window ledge in her nightgown. Mary, far more than any other sitcom heroine, Maude Findlay and Edith Bunker included, was a grown-up. The things that hassled her—the embarrassments and small calamities that muddled her days—were exactly the sort of mishaps that could plague any reasonably intelligent human being. Mary gave a dinner party and served six portions of veal—Lou Grant tried to eat three of them. Chuckles the clown died and Mary couldn't stop laughing at his funeral. When Betty Ford phoned, Mary thought it was a crank caller.

During the weekly round of rehearsals, script revisions went on constantly. Mary was generous: she supplied fresh fruit daily for the whole cast to munch on—and, unlike some television stars, she had no problem sharing the camera with other actors. Her main thought was *the show;* she wanted it to be the best—the absolute best. If it meant boosting someone else's part and trimming down her own that week, Mary was all for it. (She never counted lines to see who had the most dialogue.) And she always strove for honesty in the scripts. She knew that, in the long run, the cheap joke—the surefire laugh—wasn't half as important as the real moment. But sometimes achieving those "real moments" meant throwing out entire scripts—and rewriting from scratch—after the first rehearsal. Mary and her crew got perfection. The writers sometimes got headaches.

Tempers rarely flared on the set—not that Mary and everybody else didn't have queen- and king-size egos. Ed Asner's theory is that if you put enough big egos together, you wind up with an explosion that's either brilliant or cataclysmic. In this case, brilliance won out. By the end of the first season, Gavin MacLeod and Ted Knight were actually giving each other unasked-for acting tips—without anyone taking offense—and Gavin, Ted, Ed Asner, and their wives were a regular Saturday-night dinner group.

Mary was friendly, but she didn't socialize much. Her only contact with the other women on the show was during lunch hour when she ran a daily dance and aerobics class. It was one of the few ways in which Mary chose to exert her authority as the star. The cast and crew always broke for lunch by twelve-thirty, when the class started—rarely before, never after. Mary didn't like her exercise schedule tampered with.

The exercise, of course, was a must for her as a diabetic —and so was laying off sweets. Valerie Harper shared those same health concerns, but for a different reason—she was trying to keep her weight down. Val weighed 150 pounds when she joined *MTM* in 1970, but by the time she checked out to do her own series four years later, she was 30 pounds lighter. Mary's influence undoubtedly had a lot to do with her success. Out of necessity, Valerie and Mary policed each other. "There was a big cookie jar shaped like a pumpkin on the set," Valerie recalls. "The stagehands used to keep it filled with Oreos, Lorna Doones, the kind of crap that Wasp mothers keep on hand for kiddie snacks. Mary with her diabetes and me with my weight problems, we used to love to open that jar and just sniff the sugary smell. We'd say, 'Oh, wow!' then put the lid back on."

That was about as close to "horsing around" as the cast ever came. On *The Mary Tyler Moore Show*, the operative word was light, not loose. At a cast luncheon, someone once gave Ed Asner a stuffed animal; the message on the card read, "In your honor, a bear like this has been planted in Israel." Ted Knight was probably the closest thing *MTM* had to a resident jester; he liked to serenade Mary by humming a few bars from the Miss America theme song when she arrived on the set in the morning. She never minded that kind of teasing—in fact, she seemed to enjoy it—but practical jokes were strictly forbidden. Mary once heard about some of the antics that used to go on backstage at *M*A*S*H*—where actors regularly found their dressing rooms painted purple and their shoelaces stolen just for the fun of it—and she was shocked.

If the *MTM* group kept a rather tight rein on themselves,

it's probably because they were all serious people at heart. What bound them together as a company, more than anything, was their intense zeal for perfection. After fifteen years in show business, Mary had finally hooked up with a group of die-hard overachievers just like herself. No wonder they carried home a wagonful of Emmies every season —Mary, Ed Asner, the writers, the producers, Grant Tinker, practically everyone associated with the show seemed to have an overwhelming reverence for winning.

Whether or not the cast admitted it—or even acknowledged it to themselves—the atmosphere on *MTM* was more competitive than on any other show in town. If Valerie Harper won three Emmies in a row, Cloris Leachman countered by grabbing an Academy Award for her supporting performance in 1971's *The Last Picture Show*. Not to be outdone, Ed Asner proved he could do prize-winning headstands as a dramatic actor, too. In 1976, he won his first Emmy away from *The Mary Tyler Moore Show* for his role as the hateful father in *Rich Man, Poor Man*. A year later, he repeated that triumph and captured another Emmy for his portrayal of the slave-ship captain in *Roots*.

Shifting gears into serious drama wasn't hard for Ed Asner or Cloris Leachman. Both were far more experienced in that medium than in situation comedy. In his pre-*MTM* career, Ed had carved out an anonymous (but fairly lucrative) niche for himself playing cops and criminals— working both sides of the law, so to speak. Cloris, too, was known mainly for dramatic work, both in films and theater.

Actually, the only cast members with a substantial sit-com background were Betty White, Gavin MacLeod, and Mary herself. Gavin had played Happy Haines on *McHale's Navy* for two years and Betty (who joined the *MTM* cast in 1973) had done two comedy shows of her own in the 1950s. "I've gone from virtuous to vulturous," she quipped, and no one would argue that she'd certainly come a long way from her days as a blissful bride on the 1957 sitcom *A Date with the Angels*. *Angelic* was hardly a word you'd use to describe Sue Ann Nivens, "The Happy Homemaker"— *bitchy* and *witchy* hit closer to home!

Betty White was probably the cast member with the most television experience of all. Back in the summer of 1955, when Mary was still dancing on Hotpoint stoves, Betty was already starring on a quiz show called *Make the Connection*. At the opposite end of the spectrum were TV newcomers like Valerie Harper and Georgia Engel. Ted Knight had never been a regular on a TV series before, but he'd been knocking around Hollywood a long time—and *The Mary Tyler Moore Show* had nearly slipped through his hands, too. To Jim Brooks and Allan Burns, Ted seemed perfect casting—right from the first audition—as WJM's slightly tarnished answer to Eric Sevareid. But the network kept insisting on a younger, more appealing, better-known actor for the role.

"What's he done?" the network demanded.

"He's a former ventriloquist," was the MTM answer.

"Well, can't you get a Lyle Waggoner or James Brolin type?"

"We don't want Lyle Waggoner or James Brolin. We want this guy. He's very real and very good."

At one point, Brooks joked to Burns that maybe they should try speaking to CBS in another language—French perhaps—because they obviously weren't making much progress in English.

CBS hoped that turning Ted Baxter into a muscle-bound young hunk would lead to a Ted-and-Mary romance, which certainly wouldn't hurt the ratings.

"Ted and Mary together—it'll be the greatest thing since canned laughter. Just think about it."

"What's so great about canned laughter?"

A hush fell over the conference room—and Jim Brooks and Allan Burns nearly quit *The Mary Tyler Moore Show* before it ever aired.

Ultimately, of course, after the requisite number of memos and migraine tablets had been handed back and forth, Mary and her team won that battle. Not only did Ted Baxter emerge on-screen with all his pomposity and foolishness intact, but he stayed spartanly unattached until midway through the show's seven-year run, when Georgette Franklin arrived. She was soft-spoken and slightly empty-headed and so full of year-round Christmas spirit that she could make even Mary cringe. Georgette started out as Rhoda's befuddled friend from Rumplemayer's department store and eventually—after one of the longest courtships in TV history—became Mrs. Ted Baxter. Georgia Engel, who immortalized Ted's better half, was hardly an experienced TV performer, but Mary became her champion from her first day on the set. "I remembered how I was when I started on *Dick Van Dyke*," Mary later said. "Let's face it, I was nervous as anything. There I was, surrounded by all these pros and hoping I wouldn't miss my mark, or ruin my makeup, or forget my lines. Well, Georgia reminded me of *me*. She was trying so hard and she was really very good. Right from the start, her timing was impeccable, and the way she delivered her lines in that wispy, little-girl voice of hers just knocked us all out. How could we pass her up?"

Everyone had advice for Georgia, although not all of it was strictly serious. Cloris Leachman, who had first been unleashed on prime-time America as one of the numerous mothers on *Lassie,* warned her never to work with any animal who got a better dressing room than hers. (Cloris, a health-food fiend, also spent a great deal of her time on the set trying to interest people in yogurty desserts and alfalfa sprouts.)

As *The Mary Tyler Moore Show*'s popularity grew among sophisticates on both coasts, guest-starring roles became something of a Hollywood status symbol. It was like driving the right sports car or wearing the right labels. Working on other television shows might get you into the Polo Lounge, but an appearance on *MTM* guaranteed you a table with high visibility. Over the years, some very impressive names wound their way through the credits: Jack Cassidy played Ted Baxter's superconfident brother; Nanette Fabray and Bill Quinn were Mary's parents; and Eileen Heckart was Mary's aunt, Flo Meredith, the prize-winning newspaperwoman who could drink Lou under the table and still steal his heart. John Amos, who played Gordy the weatherman, left the newsroom in 1974 to star in his own situation-comedy series, *Good Times*; and both Valerie Harper and Cloris Leachman went on to do their own spinoffs, *Rhoda* and *Phyllis*.

Some of the show's semi-regulars created the most unforgettable characters of all: Joyce Bulifant was Murray's very dependent wife, Marie; Lisa Gerritsen played Phyllis's surprisingly mature daughter, Bess; and Priscilla Morrill was Edie Grant, the woman who walked out on Lou after thirty years of marriage.

Henry Winkler made one of his earliest TV appearances as the uninvited guest (who sat in the corner) at Mary's veal Prince Orloff party; and Penny Marshall played Mary's neighbor, Paula Kovacs, for a full season just before *Laverne and Shirley* went on the air. Even Johnny Carson did a brief walk-on—or rather a talk-on. He appeared in voice only at another one of Mary's calamity-ridden parties; this one took place during a blackout.

The success of *The Mary Tyler Moore Show* led to the birth

of a whole family of MTM sitcoms. In 1972, Grant's company, MTM Enterprises, began to branch out by launching *The Bob Newhart Show* (it aired right after Mary on Saturday night); then in 1974 came *Rhoda* and *Paul Sand in Friends and Lovers*. By that time, the MTM corporation was grossing $20 million a year and boasted five hundred people on the payroll. Mary may have been on the letterhead, and she was obviously MTM's most valuable property, but Grant was the power behind all the thrones. "He was the president," Mary recalls. "It was strictly his company. He named it after me the way some men name their boats after their wives."

Not everything that Grant and MTM tinkered with turned to gold. *Phyllis* (launched in 1975) did moderately well, but *The Texas Wheelers*—a show about a widower and his four kids living a hard-luck life on the prairie—didn't make it. (The show had one memorable footnote, however —it marked the debut of future *Star Wars* hero Mark Hamill.) *The Bob Crane Show*—originally titled *Second Start*— did even worse. It premiered in March 1975 and was canceled three months later.

All through the 1970s, MTM Enterprises continued to grow, creating such winners and losers as *Doc*, *Three for the Road*, *We've Got Each Other*, *The Tony Randall Show*, and *The Betty White Show*, to mention just a few ventures. Along with *All in the Family*'s Norman Lear, Grant Tinker was now considered a prime orchestrator of tasteful, intelligent programming on television. His style of comedy—short on belly laughs, but long on thoughtful humor—was the wave of the future.

MTM had a proven success formula that many people tried later to imitate. Invariably, each show had a star (Mary Tyler Moore, Bob Newhart, Tony Randall) backed up by a rich ensemble of zany supporting players. On

Rhoda, Valerie Harper was blessed with a depressing sister (Julie Kavner), interfering mother (Nancy Walker), hard-hat husband (David Groh), plus a slew of married and unmarried weirdo girlfriends. Bob Newhart's resident oddballs were his neighbors and group-therapy patients. Tony Randall, who played a widowed judge, had a feisty housekeeper, a prudish secretary, a nosy court reporter, and two hip and slightly hyper kids.

Another MTM trademark, of course, was the geographical locale. Pre-MTM, most situation comedies were set in New York, Los Angeles, or some never-quite-defined suburb. *The Mary Tyler Moore Show* broke that pattern by plunking its characters down in Minneapolis and using real backdrops of the city to help set the scene. Later, *The Bob Newhart Show* gave us a slice of upper-middle-class Chicago life, *Rhoda* depicted the Grand Concourse and Manhattan's less-than-elegant West Side, *Phyllis* took place in San Francisco, *Friends and Lovers* in Boston, and *The Tony Randall Show* in Philadelphia.

Although Mary was still listed as the chairman of the board, her involvement with the company remained nil. "Mary doesn't try to take over this desk and I don't try to tell her how to act," Grant Tinker informed the press. "I can't possibly do what she does and she doesn't want to do what I do, so we travel different roads toward the same end." That end, of course, was the success of MTM Enterprises. Together, Mary's talent and Grant's expertise had built the company from a one-show operation into a multimillion-dollar production empire. By the mid-1970s, MTM was supplying the three major networks with as many new shows each season as Paramount and Universal. In 1976, three MTM shows—*Rhoda*, *Phyllis*, and *Mary Tyler Moore*—all finished up in the Nielsen Top 20. Grant's winning streak was so strong that he was one of the few men who could sell the network on a new show, sight unseen, before the pilot was even made. He had become one of the most powerful men in Hollywood.

And Grant was right. He and Mary were working "toward the same end"—that is, as long as *The Mary Tyler Moore Show* continued to run. But once that show ended, would Mary's goals still be the same as her husband's?

"How will you make it on your own?" That was the very first line of Mary's TV theme song, "Love Is All Around." Mary Richards had faced that prospect—and made it on her own—in 1970. Seven years later, Mary Tyler Moore was getting ready to do the same thing.

❧ 6 ❧

Hiatus

It had to end sometime—and in February 1977 the lights in the WJM newsroom went out for the last time. After seven years, America's prime-time sweetheart was surrendering her crown and scepter. Next season *The Jeffersons* would be movin' on up to her Saturday-night time slot, although, hopefully, somewhere, on some channel, at some inconvenient hour of the day or night, Mary would continue to shine in reruns forever.

The shock was enormous. All of us who loved Mary—men and women alike, followers of feminism as well as followers of Phyllis Schlafly—felt like we'd lost a best friend. Gloria Steinem half-jokingly threatened to stage a protest at the gates of CBS; other less celebrated fans bombarded the studio with letters, postcards, and telegrams demanding a stay of execution. The network itself reportedly offered Mary something "between the moon and New York City" to reconsider.

But Mary remained firm in her decision not to stick around for an eighth season. She wanted to go while the going was good, while her show was still a winner, with her ratings and popularity intact. Why wait around for Mary Richards to become old hat, as she inevitably must? Besides, how long could Mary possibly keep playing a zippy thirtyish bachelor girl? Even by the vaguest prime-time calculations, her credentials as a young single were starting to wear thin. Mary Richards was now thirty-seven. What else could she do while waiting for Mr. Right that she hadn't already done? Learn to hang-glide, maybe.

It was time to move on. When the 168th and final episode was completed, Mary gave a small party for the cast—and then everyone dispersed with surprisingly little sadness or separation anxiety. There wasn't much reason for weeping into the champagne because most of the group didn't expect to be idle for very long. Starting in September, Gavin MacLeod would be trying out his sea legs as captain of *The Love Boat* and Ed Asner would be launching his sixty-minute dramatic series, *Lou Grant*. In Ted Knight's brand-new sitcom, he'd be playing the suave head of a female escort service. (Although CBS didn't have a fall time slot lined up for *The Ted Knight Show*, the network was definitely eyeing it as a mid-season replacement.) Meanwhile, Georgia Engel was all set to play Betty White's second banana on the new *Betty White Show*. In the show-within-a-show format, Betty would be a bitchy, divorced actress who stars in her own version of *Police Woman* and Georgia would be her ditzy roommate.

While all these projects looked promising, at least on paper, it seemed doubtful that any of them could match *The Mary Tyler Moore Show* in style or substance. When the gang trooped out of the newsroom that final time, everybody knew that a door was closing on a unique era in situation comedy. James Brooks summed it up perfectly when he said, "Not one of us believes he will ever again be part of something as special."

But would the show have stayed as "special" if Mary had chosen to hang on for a few more seasons? No, invariably the magic would have worn off—and that's why Mary was wise to leave when she did. In future seasons, Mary might have been promoted, moved into a splashier apartment, maybe even found a man, but those changes wouldn't have been enough to keep the series from falling on hard times. In 1977, the wolves were already at the door—Mary seemed to sense that—and her brand of urbane, sophisticated comedy was rapidly becoming doomed to extinction.

More and more, what Americans hungered for in their nightly TV entertainment was a quick fix—no thinking involved, please. Shows that featured violence, car crashes, and lots of "jiggle" were taking over. Even before Mary Tyler Moore pulled the plug on her series, bubble-gum farces like *Three's Company* and *Laverne and Shirley* were starting to dominate the airwaves. With America's taste in comedy at such a low ebb, even established hits like *Rhoda* and *Phyllis* were quickly losing their foothold. *Phyllis* was canceled after two seasons, due to low ratings; *Rhoda* would be gone before the end of the decade.

When she left the weekly-series grind in 1977, Mary decided a cooling-off period was in order. Comedy styles, like skirt lengths and hairdos, seemed to run in cycles; eventually, she believed, audiences would tire of bingeing on junk programming and grow hungry for more substantial material again. She'd wait till then to think about another TV series.

In the meantime, Mary didn't have to worry about other offers. Made-for-television movies, feature films, another stab at theater acting perhaps—it all loomed enticingly before her. Mary Tyler Moore wasn't simply a star anymore—she was a superstar. During the 1970s, when Marlo Thomas, Barbara Parkins, and so many other promising newcomers of the 1960s had faded into virtual oblivion, Mary had emerged as a major figure in the entertainment world. In Hollywood now, all you had to say was *Mary*.

Everyone knew exactly who you meant—and it wasn't Mary Steenburgen or Mary Kay Place.

On the personal side, Mary didn't seem to have any worries, either, at least none that were visible. Her health was reasonably good, her diabetes was in control, and her marriage was more secure than ever. Her son Richie was twenty years old and a little on the wild side, but that was pretty much par for the course with kids these days, wasn't it? In time, "he'd find himself " and settle down—they all did eventually.

As she said goodbye to *The Mary Tyler Moore Show*, just a few months shy of her fortieth birthday, Mary seemed to be heading into the most promising decade of her life. She had finally put all her demons behind her. Her prospects looked so good that her biographer Chris Bryars wrote in *The Real Mary Tyler Moore:* "What has happened in Mary's life typifies the American dream in the Seventies. Skeptics are likely to say that that's no longer possible, but Mary Tyler Moore has survived, and because of the lessons learned and the maturity gained, there seem to be no obstacles on the horizon."

As it turned out, nothing could be farther from the truth.

7

Variety Is Not the Spice of Life

Mary spent most of 1977 sleeping late in the morning and trying to decide what to do with her life. For the first time in more years than she cared to remember, she was a lady of leisure. She had few appointments to keep, no early makeup calls to worry about, no scripts to learn. At first, it was seventh heaven; but after a while Mary grew bored with a daily routine that was basically no routine.

She was too much of a workaholic to simply drop out. She straightened her closets, did crossword puzzles, took voice and dancing lessons, and played endless sets of tennis. Mostly she was standing still and she knew it. Her one venture back into television—a musical special called "Mary's Incredible Dream"—didn't set the Nielsen ratings on fire. But Mary didn't read anything dire into that one little setback—she certainly wasn't ready to retire permanently! No, maybe it was just time to give television a rest for a while and pick up other threads of her career again.

Mary was anxious to try her hand at straight dramatic roles—maybe even take another stab at the movies. But the world of motion pictures wasn't exactly waiting to welcome her back with open arms. In 1969, when Mary left Universal, she was thirty-two years old. Now she was forty

—and forty-year-old actresses were hardly a hot commodity in Hollywood. In the late 1970s, even established film stars like Glenda Jackson and Liza Minnelli occasionally went begging for work. Nobody was writing roles for Princess Leia's mother. Ever since the 1960s, movies had been dominated by men. It was still the buddy-buddy era of Redford and Newman in *The Sting*, Mark Hamill and Harrison Ford in *Star Wars*, Walter Matthau and George Burns in *The Sunshine Boys*. Women weren't considered a key part of the package when big movie deals were put together; and some box-office movers like Al Pacino and Dustin Hoffman could make film after film without any leading ladies at all. The few juicy roles that did exist for women over thirty were quickly swallowed up by Jane Fonda, Diane Keaton, and Faye Dunaway. Outsiders like Mary Tyler Moore hardly stood a chance.

The shame of it was that Mary was labeled as a *television actress*—and few movie directors could envision her doing anything beyond the thirty-minute confines of situation comedy. Take a movie like *The Turning Point*. Mary would have been perfect as Shirley MacLaine's foil—Emma, the aging ballerina—but director Herb Ross insisted on an actress with impressive dramatic credentials. Even though Mary would have been far more believable in the dance sequences, Anne Bancroft, who played the role, had films like *The Miracle Worker*, *The Pumpkin Eater*, and *The Graduate* to her credit.

Mary ran into the same trouble with *Same Time, Next Year*. For a while, she was rumored to be a serious contender for the role that Ellen Burstyn had created on Broadway, but in the end Ellen wound up doing the screen version herself. Ellen was simply a safer choice as far as the studio was concerned. She had cinematic respectability (an Oscar for *Alice Doesn't Live Here Anymore*) plus box-office popularity following her appearance in the enormously successful horror film *The Exorcist*. Moreover, with Alan Alda set as the leading man, Mary's television background once again worked against her. The studio worried that teaming the *M*A*S*H* star with Mary Richards might lower *Same Time, Next Year* to the level of a made-for-TV movie. Why should audiences pay to see Alan and Mary on screen when they could catch him on *M*A*S*H* every Monday night, while Mary was everywhere in reruns both as Laura Petrie and Mary Richards? Ludicrous as it sounds, that's what most movie executives believed in 1977. It wasn't until *Welcome Back, Kotter* graduate John Travolta turned the movie world on its ear in *Saturday Night Fever* that the movie studios began to acknowledge the big-screen potential of small-screen performers.

Aside from *The Turning Point* and *Same Time, Next Year*, what other scripts might have matched Mary's talent? Well, Neil Simon was writing some interesting comedy roles for women—and Mary would have been a natural as Richard Dreyfuss's reluctant roommate in *The Goodbye Girl* or James Caan's leading lady in *Chapter Two*. But in those days Simon only scripted screenplays with one actress in mind—his wife, Marsha Mason.

Should Mary turn her sights back to TV? She was determined not to launch another situation comedy series too soon—*The Mary Tyler Moore Show* had barely been laid to rest—and the dramatic side of prime time (at least as far as weekly series were concerned) didn't look much more promising. Somehow Mary couldn't quite see herself skirting danger in designer jeans like one of *Charlie's Angels*. And she was hardly the homespun pioneer type like Caroline Ingalls or Olivia Walton.

Ultimately, Mary found a project that appealed to her. She had read *First, You Cry*—an autobiographical account

of TV newswoman Betty Rollin's bout with cancer and
breast surgery and her difficult road to recovery. Mary felt
it would make an excellent TV dramatization, and MTM
Enterprises secured the rights for her. In the two-hour
television opus Mary was surrounded by a formidable cast.
Anthony Perkins played Betty's husband, Florence El-
dridge was her mother, and Richard Crenna was cast as the
man Betty turns to, following her mastectomy, when her
marriage falls apart.

Mary began work on *First, You Cry* nearly a year after
taping the last episode of *The Mary Tyler Moore Show,* and
she was more than anxious to be back on a soundstage
again. She looked terrific and felt refreshed, but apparently
she had had it up to here with enforced relaxation! "How
much tennis can you play?" she jokingly asked reporters on
the day that MTM announced plans to turn Betty Rollin's
best-selling book into a dramatic television special.

"Thank God Mary's out of the house," her husband
Grant added with a slight grin that seemed to imply more
than it said.

It was obvious why *First, You Cry*—the story of a woman
trying to rebuild her life after a devastating illness—held
such fascination for Mary. She found it easy to identify
with Betty Rollin because her own battle with diabetes had
been something of a similar journey. Beginning in the late
1970s, Mary seemed to have an almost obsessive interest in
plays and film scripts that focused on some kind of illness
or handicap. In *Whose Life Is It, Anyway?* she would portray
a woman paralyzed from the neck down; in *Six Weeks,* the
mother of a young girl dying of leukemia; in *Heartsounds,*
the wife of a terminal cardiac patient. A psychologist might
contend that Mary was still trying to confront her own
demons by choosing these projects; that this morbid preoc-
cupation with medical drama was a kind of exorcism. Mary

claimed that she simply chose the most intriguing projects available—and illness just happens to make good drama.

For the first time in her career Mary was playing a real person, but before going into production she didn't spend a great deal of time with Betty Rollin. And although *First, You Cry* was filmed on location in New York, Betty only visited the set once. If she'd wanted to, she probably could have watched the production right from her own office window. Many of the film's exterior scenes were shot right outside 30 Rockefeller Center—the building where Betty still worked as an NBC correspondent.

Betty kept her involvement in the film down to a minimum. She didn't help write the screenplay for the two-hour TV presentation—or exercise any creative control over the final cut—but her faith in Mary Tyler Moore and producer Philip Barry was amply justified. When Betty saw a screening of *First, You Cry,* she was pleased with the entire film and especially enthusiastic about Mary's performance. She had only one small complaint: on screen Mary and Anthony Perkins did most of their talking—and bickering—in the Herzog family dining room. "We never had a dining room in that apartment," Betty confided. "That was purely a Hollywood invention."

One of the supporting roles—that of Betty's friend, Anne—went to Philip Barry's wife, Patricia. In the early 1970s she had played Addie Olsen Williams, one of the most beloved heroines of *Days of Our Lives.* Working with her, Mary got an instant education in the power of the daytime soaps. On several occasions, fans came running up to Patricia Barry in the street, waving their autograph books and screaming, "Addie! Addie! Why did they let you die!" (Patricia's character had come to a rather brutal and apparently unjust end on *Days of Our Lives.*) These fans couldn't have cared less that they were standing just a few feet away from Mary Tyler Moore, Richard Crenna, and Anthony Perkins. The sight of their adored Addie—magically restored to life before their very eyes—was all that enthralled them.

Mary found *First, You Cry* a more challenging and demanding project than anything she had ever done. Ultimately, it was a more satisfying work experience, too. The film's focal problem—mastectomy and its emotional aftermath—was indeed a difficult subject to present, and Mary tried to do it with sensitivity and honesty. It forced her to dig far below the surface of her own psyche to find colors and emotions for this role that no acting experience had ever demanded of her before. It was an incredibly draining role that sapped all of her strength, both emotionally and physically.

But events in her own life—even more agonizing than the material she was playing on screen—soon took precedence. Mary was still in New York, midway through filming *First, You Cry,* when word came that her 21-year-old sister, Elizabeth Ann, had died of an apparent drug overdose. Mary was stunned by the news. She refused to accept the possibility that her sister might have taken her own life.

Filming on *First, You Cry* shut down as Mary flew home to Los Angeles for the funeral. At the airport, Grant and Mary, both too grief-stricken to speak, shunned reporters. Grant's only comment was, "It's a private family matter."

According to James Kono, an investigator in the Los Angeles County coroner's office, an autopsy revealed "pulmonary edema, a lung condition that is consistent with someone who has taken an overdose."

Mary's aunt, Alberta Hackett, told the press, "The poor girl died of a heart seizure. Can't you leave it at that?"

Elizabeth's death left Mary badly shaken. They were so far apart in age it had been practically impossible for them to be close in a sisterly way; now they would never bridge that gap. When Elizabeth was a toddler, Mary was already married, out of the house, raising a child of her own, and launching a TV career. In a way, Mary was more like an aunt than a big sister. Ironically, in 1978, they were just reaching a point in both their lives when a closeness between them might have finally developed—now that Elizabeth was an adult and working part-time in television herself. At the time of her death, Elizabeth was attending Los Angeles City College and working at KNXT-TV's news bureau on weekends. Shortly before she died, she had broken up with her boyfriend.

"She was going with a young man," Mary later told journalist Aaron Gold, "and the relationship was coming to an end. She was sedating herself, taking Darvon, and she took too many and she also had two drinks that night and —she died. That's the story of that. She was a wonderful, wonderful girl and she was not a drug taker. . . . It was a mistake."

After the funeral, Mary returned to New York to finish work on *First, You Cry.* When it aired as a two-hour movie on November 8, 1978, the critical and popular acclaim represented a stunning success for Mary. Later, the film received four Emmy nominations, including a nomination for Mary as Best Actress in a Dramatic Special.

On the other hand, Mary's second attempt in the musical/variety arena had hit a sour note. On February 22, 1978 (barely a week after her sister's funeral), the sequel to her last musical outing, "Mary's Incredible Dream," had aired. It was called "How to Survive the 70s and Maybe Even Bump into Happiness." The show neither survived the Nielsens nor bumped into critical acclaim. Why did it fail? Certainly, it was the kind of project that looked good on paper. For her two leading men, Mary borrowed Harvey

Korman from *The Carol Burnett Show* and John Ritter from *Three's Company*. Together they glibly poked fun at compulsive tennis players, group therapy, how-to books, singles bars, and jogging, but the humor didn't exactly produce belly laughs and guffaws. The skits tried to be with-it—perhaps a little too with-it—but somehow satire just wasn't Mary's style. Her antics were sophisticated, yet tame compared to the outrageous shenanigans on *Saturday Night Live*. Without a character to step into—and the security of a regular situation comedy plot—Mary was lost at sea, a ship without an anchor.

For seven years on *The Mary Tyler Moore Show*, Mary had possessed a golden touch: she had known how to make people laugh and how to keep audiences hooked. Now all the variety specials she tried foundered in the ratings. Where had her vast following of viewers gone? They obviously missed Mary—at least the Mary they had once known—but apparently they weren't willing to foresake *Starsky and Hutch* to find out "How to Survive the 70s and Maybe Even Bump into Happiness." In three key cities—New York, Chicago, and Los Angeles—ABC's *Starsky and Hutch* clobbered Mary's show on CBS, although she did pull slightly ahead of NBC's *Police Woman* with Angie Dickinson.

During Easter week of 1978, Mary made another brief TV appearance. She co-hosted CBS's fiftieth-anniversary salute "CBS: On the Air" with Walter Cronkite. The fact that CBS chose Mary to emcee this splashy, star-studded gala was a definite reiteration of the network's faith in her. They might have chosen Lucille Ball, Carol Burnett, Michael Learned, Jean Stapleton, or Valerie Harper, but somehow the selection of Mary seemed just right. Despite her few false musical steps, she remained the premiere star in the CBS galaxy.

By the fall of 1978, Mary was ready to return to weekly TV. CBS was anxious for her to do a new situation-comedy series—so anxious that they probably would have approved any story idea she insisted on—but Mary wasn't interested. She had her heart set on doing a musical/variety hour and nothing could persuade her to change her mind. In all fairness, Mary had some valid reasons for ruling out a situation-comedy reprise: her type of low-keyed, thoughtful humor was no longer in vogue on prime time; she could never hope to create another character as unique and appealing as Mary Richards; and why should viewers become attached to her in a new comedy series when they could still watch her old show in reruns?

By the same token, why should viewers watch her slosh through a sentimental hour of song and dance every week? Her two variety specials hadn't garnered large audiences. But on Mary's part it was no longer a purely logical decision. The plain truth was that Mary was tired of the sitcom circuit. And after all her failures as a musical entertainer, she was still obsessed with proving that she could sell herself to the American public as a latter-day Ginger Rogers. The recent low ratings of her specials hadn't discouraged her in the least—far from it. They fueled her ambition even more.

Mary, after all, was the girl whose whole life had been wrapped up in dancing since the age of four, the girl who declared repeatedly, "In school, I never cared about studying math or history or much of anything else. What would I ever need those things for? I was going to be a dancer, and nothing else mattered." And no matter what pinnacles of success she reached as an actress, an underlying frustration remained. Mary often told reporters, "No matter how far my career has gone, I've always felt I never achieved what I set out to do. I can't help it. To my dying day, I'll think of myself not as a successful actress, but as a failed dancer.''

Mary never forgot *Breakfast at Tiffany's* and the humiliation she suffered at the hands of those preview audiences. Now, for the first time in her career, she was truly in a position to call the shots. She had the power of her own company, MTM Enterprises, behind her. If CBS wanted her back, the only way they could get her was top hat, cane, tap shoes, and all.

Mary's new variety show was simply called *Mary*—and that may have been the first sign of trouble. Apparently, no one in the MTM think tank could come up with a more catchy title. Someone had suggested *The New Mary Tyler Moore Show*, but that was nixed for obvious reasons. Viewers might mistakenly believe they were about to see new episodes of Mary Richards in Minneapolis. Furthermore, everyone remembered what a lukewarm reception viewers gave Dick Van Dyke when he called his second series *The New Dick Van Dyke Show*. As Mary herself asked at one early production meeting, "What happens when the show isn't new anymore? Do we change the title again—and to what?"

Other discarded titles ranged from cute to campy to worse: *The Musical Side of Mary, Here's Mary, An Evening with Mary* and *Mary and Her Friends.* Another rejected title was *Mary Tyler Moore: On Her Own.* On reflection, it might have worked. The idea came from the lyric of her old TV theme song, "Love Is All Around," and the line it sprang from was "How will you make it on your own?" In this series, Mary would indeed be on her own, without her old cohorts (Ed Asner, Ted Knight, and Gavin MacLeod) and without a comfortable screen persona like Mary Richards to fall back on.

But *Mary Tyler Moore: On Her Own* was passed over in favor of just plain *Mary*—and CBS assigned the show an eight-to-nine-P.M. time slot on Sunday night. With an equal amount of fanfare and foreboding, *TV Guide* announced: "Fresh from her conquest of the situation-comedy world, Mary Tyler Moore is now tackling a format that has been the undoing of countless accomplished performers: the variety hour."

Mary promised that her format would be more "intimate" and "less razzle-dazzle" than the run-of-the-mill entertainment hour, but even so it was a high-risk venture. The list of casualties on the comedy/variety scene was frightening enough to strike terror into the hearts of many seasoned performers. During the 1960s and '70s, variety shows came and went about as quickly as one of Liz Taylor's marriages. And for the stars of such shows defeat was particularly humiliating. If a sitcom or dramatic series failed, perhaps it was a badly written or badly conceived idea; there are usually scriptwriters to blame and a whole slew of supporting actors. But on a variety show, success or failure rests on the shoulders of a single person—*the star* —whose personality will either charm an audience or chase an audience away.

The hallowed halls of prime-time TV were filled with more than enough ghosts to give Mary pause. Leslie Uggams's CBS variety show had premiered on September 28, 1969, and was canceled on December 14 of the same year. Tim Conway's show debuted the following September and was also a pre-Christmas casualty. In September 1972 ABC gave a green light to *The Julie Andrews Hour*. Each week Julie recreated one of her immortal moments in *My Fair Lady*, *Mary Poppins*, or *The Sound of Music*; and if clowning around wasn't exactly Julie's strong suit, she had Rich Little and Alice Ghostley on hand to round out the comedy skits. But the show barely limped through the winter and was permanently laid to rest in April.

Other short-lived variety shows included *Bobbie Gentry's Happiness Hour*, *The Mac Davis Show*, and *The Captain and Tennille*. Even *Tony Orlando and Dawn*, one of the more successful prime-time music hours, only hung in for a little over two seasons. It wasn't that viewers seemed to prefer one style of music to another, either. Rock singers failed as variety hosts; so did country-western stars and Broadway names. And if musical superstars like Mac Davis couldn't crack the TV variety scene, what hope did Mary Tyler Moore have? As a musical performer, she barely had any identity at all.

Nevertheless, Mary plowed ahead. For her new show, she chose six regulars—Dick Shawn, James Hampton, Swoosie Kurtz, David Letterman, Michael Keaton, and Judy Kahan—to back her up in the comedy department. And even though Mary was destined to fall on her face with this shaky project, no one would contest the fact that she definitely had an eye for picking talent. Just as all the supporting players on *The Mary Tyler Moore Show* had blossomed into stars, most of this group later went on to bigger and better things, too. David Letterman got his own show on NBC; Swoosie Kurtz co-starred with Tony Randall in *Love, Sidney* and won a Tony for her Broadway role in *Fifth of July*; and Michael Keaton became a box-office top banana in film comedies like *Mr. Mom* and *Night Shift*.

Considering the enormous amount of talent gathered together for this show, it's mind-boggling that *Mary* still managed to fail so fast and furiously. Certainly the time slot was a severe handicap. CBS scheduled *Mary* on Sunday night opposite two potential blockbusters—ABC's *Battlestar Galactica* and NBC's *The Big Event*. *Battlestar Galactica* —TV's first space-age soap opera—gave viewers a little dose of *Star Wars* every week. There were evil Cylons, handsome young space heroes (Richard Hatch and Dirk

Benedict), a wise old starfleet commander (Lorne Greene), and all kinds of dazzling galactic gadgetry (the special effects were dreamed up by *Star Wars* wizard John Dykstra). For more down-to-earth viewers, NBC's first *Big Event*—"Centennial"—was a surefire entertainment bet. Based on the James Michener bestseller, "Centennial" was a rip-roaring adventure saga that recreated one hundred years of American history. It also featured an all-star cast that included Robert Conrad, Richard Chamberlain, Raymond Burr, Clint Walker, Sally Kellerman, Chad Everett, and Chief Dan George. On her new show, Mary had vetoed the idea of guest stars entirely.

How could Mary possibly compete with the "Centennial" pageantry and *Battlestar* pyrotechnics? Her ideas seemed frail and vulnerable beside her two bigger-than-life competitors. "One regular segment of my show," she promised, "will be a date of the week, in which I go out with a bigger and funnier loser than the week before." At that time—September 1978—Mary was almost forty-one years old. As one critic later remarked, "There wasn't anything funny about that segment, rather something sad."

Mary tried to close her eyes and wish away the competition. Rumors abounded that Mary had allowed herself to be steered into a practically hopeless time slot and her show would be massacred in the ratings in short order; but Mary herself turned a deaf ear to warnings of doom and gloom. "Oh, no, we asked for this Sunday-night time period," she maintained. "We wanted to follow directly after *60 Minutes* because we think that audience is exactly the right audience for our show."

Mary's logic was perhaps a little thin: Why in the world would an investigative news program (with a large male audience) make a strong lead-in for a light and bubbly variety show? But Mary seemed sold on the connection, even if the rest of us weren't. In July 1978, just two months before lift-off, Mary told Rick Du Brow of the *Los Angeles Herald-Examiner*: "The one thing we know about the audience that watches *60 Minutes* is that it's wide awake, and you can't say that for all audiences. And our kind of show will require some attention. You know, it's not going to be frothy. It's going to be easy to watch, but we're going to be doing grown-up material. And we want a grown-up audience."

There was, however, a flip side to that reasoning. After watching a full hour of hard news, often graphic and depressing, on *60 Minutes*, viewers might be hungry to clear their minds with pure escapism, not "grown-up entertainment." If so, *Battlestar Galactica* and *The Big Event* stood a much better chance of attracting an audience.

As it turned out, *Mary* was a major disappointment of the 1978 season. Although eight episodes were filmed, only three of them actually aired. *Mary* premiered on September 24, 1978, and was canceled right after its third telecast on October 8. CBS moved *All in the Family* and *One Day at a Time* into that Sunday-night time slot and ratings immediately picked up. In fact, by the end of the season, CBS's Sunday-night comedy lineup was able to knock *Battlestar Galactica* off the air.

Everybody had a theory as to why *Mary* didn't work. The show had no guest stars. Mary sang too much. The show should have been scheduled on Saturday nights, immediately following *Rhoda*. Or else Mary didn't sing enough. The show should have been scheduled on Monday nights between *M*A*S*H* and *Lou Grant*.

Even *The Gong Show* lasted longer. By now Mary was certainly no stranger to failure; nevertheless, this defeat was exceptionally devastating. A month later, Mary would triumph again with the telecast of *First, You Cry*—but that was a dramatic victory, not a musical one. The musical success which she hungered for so deeply continued to elude her. Moreover, *Mary* was the first TV series of hers that ever failed. It was the first time Mary had gone down in defeat on her home ground, television. Unlike the movies or Broadway, this was supposed to be her medium. Until then, CBS had assumed—and so had Mary—that her audience would stay faithful even if Mary simply chose to read the phone book on the air (although the network should have known better after the icy reception her two variety specials had received from the public). Now Mary was no longer an infallible superstar—that illusion was shattered. She was suddenly as vulnerable as anyone else on the tube. She had been lucky with *The Dick Van Dyke Show* and *The Mary Tyler Moore Show*. There was no guarantee that the magic would last forever.

As always, Mary "put on a happy face" for reporters and proceeded to fall quietly apart in private. She smiled bravely, reminding us she was still the best darn sport in Hollywood, and spoke philosophically about cancellation. She told Jeff Weingrad of the *New York Post*, "When you try new things, you take a risk. And when you take a risk, you must be prepared for failure. It's part and parcel of being an artist, of being a creative person. Sure, I'm terribly disappointed, not only for me, but for everyone involved. But you've got to be very grown up about it."

Mary, indeed, appeared so "grown up" about it that she almost had us believing she felt no pain. The strong-willed figure she presented now was a far cry from the fragile young woman who fell apart so visibly when *Breakfast at Tiffany's* closed. She was becoming Hollywood's most inspiring stoic, and nothing, it seemed, could ruffle her feathers. Other stars might stoop to tantrums in public, sink into depression, fire their managers, divorce their husbands, or lose themselves in a comforting oblivion of drugs or drink. Not Mary. She seemed immune to such antics. Her television career was at a low ebb, and her marriage to Grant was already in serious trouble, whether her friends realized it or not. But on the surface Mary remained cool and professional. The grand winner had become an equally magnificent loser.

She poured all her anger and frustration into one obsessive goal: she must return to television and make her variety show work. In March of 1979—just five months after her first debacle—Mary was back on the air again. She was still doing pirouettes and pratfalls, but with a few crucial changes. This time her show was fairly saturated with high-charisma profiles; Mary was entertaining guest stars and lots of them—Gene Kelly, Mike Douglas, Lucille Ball, Paul Williams, Nancy Walker, Bonnie Franklin, Erik Estrada—even though Mary had vetoed the guest-star concept the first time around. (By this time she had no doubt realized that even television's most successful variety queen, Carol Burnett, had relied on guest stars to round out her show.)

The new effort—redubbed *The Mary Tyler Moore Hour*—had a plot, too. In fact, MTM was billing it as a *sitvar*—a situation/variety show—which meant it was a situation comedy with a few songs and dances thrown in. The story line hinged on the idea of a show within a show. Mary played a character named Mary McKinnon, the star of a prime-time variety show, who was surrounded—to her perpetual distraction—by a producer, a head writer, a secretary, a maid, and a CBS usher. The plot of each episode was built around that week's guest star. It was hardly a revolutionary idea. On *The Jack Benny Show*, which ran for fifteen years on television, Jack played a show business personality surrounded by a wacky group of friends and co-workers. *Burns and Allen* was much the same situation. Oh, well, if it worked for them . . .

The trouble was it didn't work for Mary. Her new time slot was Sunday night at ten P.M. By then, of course, that wide-awake *60 Minutes* audience was probably dozing. Once again, Mary gathered an impressive lineup of supporting players around her: Joyce Van Patten played Mary's companion/secretary, Michael Lombard was her producer, and Michael Keaton (the only holdover from her fall fiasco) became her stage-door gofer. But the show-within-in-a-show concept didn't appeal to audiences (MTM should have realized that after the failure of *The Betty White Show* a season before), and *The Mary Tyler Moore Hour* was canceled in May.

This time Mary made her peace with the inevitable. She didn't try to tell herself that her material was too "thoughtful" or "sophisticated." She didn't promise to return in the fall with a new and improved version of her show. She simply, finally, accepted the fact that she was not cut out to be Carol Burnett. She announced with quiet but grim finality that she would never try a variety show again. "I think I've worked all that out of my system," she said. "As some journalist was kind enough to point out to me, why does a forty-year-old woman suddenly think she can become a song-and-dance man?"

Strangely, though, Mary now began lamenting the demise of her first variety show—*Mary*—which she thought was superior to the *Hour*. She blamed CBS for nipping it in the bud after only three telecasts. She told writer Aaron Gold, "It was a kind of watered-down *Saturday Night Live* —off-beat humor, black humor, very sharp humor—and I don't think the audience was ready to see me in that setting. But I think it would have worked eventually had they not been gun-shy and taken it off."

Many journalists tended to agree with Mary's analysis of the defeat. After all, neither *The Dick Van Dyke Show* nor *The Mary Tyler Moore Show* had premiered as instant Nielsen winners, yet CBS had kept the faith with both shows, giving them time to iron out the wrinkles and slowly but surely find their viewers.

At the same time, Mary confided to Gold that she "had never truly believed" in the second variety format, with its glut of guest stars and foolishly contrived storylines. Apparently, Mary had gone into the project with a feeling of doom, but anxious to placate the network and some of the powerful voices within MTM.

But was this the whole story? Or was Mary suddenly changing the tune to suit her own purposes? Back in October 1978, when *Mary* was canceled, conflicting reports had circulated in the trade papers. According to some press accounts, MTM Enterprises—not CBS—was the real villain of the piece. Allegedly CBS was willing to stick with the series and give it a little more nurturing time in the Nielsens, but Grant Tinker and Mary Tyler Moore wanted out. According to these accounts, Grant and Mary were so distressed by the first signs of failure that they demanded cancellation from CBS so they could go back to the drawing board and come up with a new project for midseason.

Were Grant and Mary really guilty of engineering the demise of their own show? On October 19, 1978, the *New York Post* reported: "Don't believe it about CBS canceling Mary Tyler Moore. MTM Enterprises actually canceled their *own* show, then persuaded CBS to let them plan their replacement. All this will cost CBS $3.2 million—indicating MTM's enormous clout, since CBS hoped to save *Mary* by simply shifting her time slot."

Whether Mary had pulled the plug on her own show or CBS had done it for her didn't really matter much in the

long haul. No matter how you sliced it, Mary had tried and
failed four times (in two specials and two variety shows) to
establish herself as a musical entertainer on TV. This last
professional blow—the cancellation of the *Hour*—created a
definite rift between star and network. Since 1961, Mary
had worked exclusively for CBS; after *The Mary Tyler Moore
Hour* fizzed out, Mary closed the door on that network. She
didn't rejoin them until 1985. Grant Tinker's association
with CBS also came to an end. He eventually became chief
executive at NBC, and in recent years a substantial number
of MTM hits—shows like *Hill Street Blues, Remington Steele,*
and *St. Elsewhere*—have all found a nest under the peacock's
feathers.

The mishandling of Mary as a variety queen wasn't
MTM's only gripe with CBS. In the late 1970s, few MTM
shows fared well on that network. In 1977, *The Betty White
Show* fell by the wayside after CBS scheduled it opposite
ABC's *Monday Night Football.* Later, both *Rhoda* and *Phyllis*
were abandoned by the network; and *Lou Grant,* a perennial Emmy winner, was canceled in 1982, allegedly because
of Edward Asner's inflammatory political stands.

As the 1970s drew to a close, it was hard for Mary to feel
welcome at CBS anymore. So much had changed. During
the first half of the decade, when shows like *Mary Tyler
Moore* and *Bob Newhart* were riding high on the prime-time
horizon, Mary and Grant and their production company
had pumped new vitality into the network. Back in the
1960s, the network had been dependent on shows like *Green
Acres, Mayberry R.F.D.,* and *The Beverly Hillbillies;* MTM
Productions had brought a new sense of style and sophistication to CBS, and Mary's imprint meant not only respectability—her shows knew how to draw ratings, too. In the
1975–76 TV season, three MTM ventures—*Phyllis, Rhoda,*
and *The Mary Tyler Moore Show*—were all in Nielsen's Top

20. And year after year, MTM programs, actors, writers, and directors snared the lion's share of Emmy awards.

But by the end of the decade that kind of prestige was no longer important. Prime time had left Mary Tyler Moore and her brand of soft-sell entertainment far behind. The network had new toys to play with—*The Dukes of Hazzard, Dallas, Knots Landing,* and a hunk named Tom Selleck. Soap operas about greedy rich folks were the latest nighttime craze. So were shows that emphasized fast cars, beautiful girls, brawls, and shoot-outs.

Like the miniskirts she wore when Mary Richards first arrived in Minneapolis, on television at least Mary Tyler Moore was now a thing of the past.

After making her TV debut as the Hotpoint Pixie, Mary got to show off her legs on Richard Diamond: Private Detective. *Pretty soon casting directors noticed that she had other assets, too. (Courtesy Sterling's Magazines, Inc.)*

For five golden years Mary Tyler
Moore and Dick Van Dyke were
America's favorite comedy couple.
The Dick Van Dyke Show
became a TV classic and brought
Mary her first Emmys. (Courtesy
Sterling's Magazines, Inc.)

In January 1962 CBS moved The
Dick Van Dyke Show from a
Tuesday to a Wednesday night
timeslot, hoping ratings would
improve. Carl Reiner, Rose Marie,
Morey Amsterdam, Larry
Mathews, Dick, and Mary helped
advertise the news. (Courtesy
Sterling's Magazines, Inc.)

During her Dick Van Dyke *years, Mary was devoted to her son, Richard Meeker, Jr., and her brand-new husband, Grant Tinker.* (Courtesy Sterling's Magazines, Inc.)

OPPOSITE: Domestic bliss was a major ingredient in Dick Van Dyke and Mary Tyler Moore's screen success. As Rob and Laura Petrie, they were New Rochelle's perennial lovebirds, but their TV son (Larry Mathews) found the comics much more fascinating than their kissing. (Courtesy Sterling's Magazines, Inc.)

ABOVE: In the 1960s Mary Tyler Moore went from one sugar-and-spice role to another with bitter results. In Thoroughly Modern Millie *she was overshadowed by Julie Andrews; in* A Change of Habit *she was miscast opposite Elvis Presley.* (Courtesy Sterling's Magazines, Inc.)

In the early 1970s Mary transformed TV comedy forever as she became bright and breezy bachelor girl, Mary Richards, a new kind of heroine, on The Mary Tyler Moore Show. *(Ron Galella)*

In 1971 Mary joined writer Cleveland Amory, Doris Day, Angie Dickinson, and other celebrities in a benefit to help save homeless animals. (Courtesy Sterling's Magazines, Inc.)

During the height of her success on The Mary Tyler Moore Show, *Mary enjoyed guesting on Dinah Shore's daytime talk hour.* (Courtesy Sterling's Magazines, Inc.)

For seven seasons Ed Asner played Mary's gruff but lovable boss, Lou Grant. It was obvious to viewers that Mary idolized Lou but the scriptwriters shied away from involving their characters romantically. (Ron Galella)

OPPOSITE: *Grant and Mary were Hollywood's idea of the perfect husband and wife. Together they built MTM Enterprises, one of the most powerful production empires in television. But by the late 1970s their personal relationship was falling apart.* (Ron Galella)

ABOVE: *In June 1980 Mary was awarded a special Tony citation for her magnificent performance in Broadway's* Whose Life Is It, Anyway? *At the awards supper, held at the New York Hilton Hotel, Ann Miller (herself a Tony nominee that night for* Sugar Babies) *stopped by to congratulate Mary.* (Ron Galella)

ABOVE: *After her divorce from Grant, Mary appeared on the New York party circuit with frequent escort Sir Gordon White.* (Ron Galella)

Michael Lindsay-Hogg, the director of Whose Life Is It, Anyway?, *also squired Mary around town.* (Ron Galella)

On March 31, 1981—just a few months after her son's tragic death—Mary bravely appeared at the Academy Award ceremonies in Los Angeles and presented the "best supporting actor" trophy to her Ordinary People co-star Timothy Hutton. (Ron Galella)

*Mary still keeps in touch with fellow thespians Ed Asner and Jean Stapleton.
During her MTM years Mary and All in the Family's Jean Stapleton were
often competing for the same Emmy. (Ron Galella)*

*Over the years Mary has grown closer to her parents, George and Marjorie Moore.
In fact, Mary's mom unwittingly played matchmaker in her daughter's romance
with Dr. Robert Levine. (Ron Galella)*

By the summer of 1982 Mary had become a real New Yorker. She frequently attended Broadway premieres, turned up regularly at posh East Side discos, and kept in shape bicycling in Central Park (Ron Galella)

ABOVE: *Mary and her third husband, Dr. Robert Levine, lead a quiet life in Manhattan. Though his schedule as a cardiologist keeps him busy, he flew to Toronto to visit with Mary when she was filming* Heartsounds *there.* (Ron Galella)

As she nears the half-century mark, Mary is getting ready to return to television in her third situation comedy series. On the basis of her past accomplishments, she is already considered one of the most influential TV actresses of our time. But Mary refuses to stop. "I'll never retire," she promises. "For me, not working is like not breathing." (Ron Galella)

⇒ 8 ⇐

Goodbye, Vanilla Madonna

What does Hollywood make you think of? Fast cars, fast food, and instant divorces. In a town where people check in and out of relationships as casually as they change hairdressers or tennis partners, only the palm trees seem riveted to one place. The knowledgeables don't wonder if a particular marriage will fail—it's a simply a question of *when*. At posh parties, you hear the ladies who look like elegant, storefront mannequins from Rodeo Drive forecast with fiendish nonchalance, "Oh, I give that couple six months" . . . or "two years" . . . or "five years" . . . "it's just a matter of time."

But Mary Tyler Moore and Grant Tinker were different —or at least they seemed to be. In May 1978—just a year and a half before their separation was publicly announced— they were still the most envied couple in Hollywood. *All in the Family* producer Norman Lear—who was MTM's chief competitor as a manufacturer of sitcoms with substance—told *McCall's* magazine that Grant and Mary were "terrific. To live in this environment and be as civilized as they are is not only conspicuous, it's a bit short of saintlike."

Yet the signs of strain had been there, even during the golden days of the early 1970s. In November 1973, right after the start of *The Mary Tyler Moore Show*'s fourth season on television, Grant and Mary had nearly canceled their marriage. He was busy expanding the MTM production empire, focusing all his energies on *The Bob Newhart Show* and the imminent birth of *Rhoda;* she was all wrapped up in sustaining the momentum of her own show. It was a question of communication—or rather noncommunication. In the midst of all this, Mary and Grant were in the process of building a magnificent beach house at Malibu. "I thought Grant wanted to live there. He thought I did," said Mary. "It turned out neither of us really wanted to be so far away from the studio. We were making the sacrifice for each other. It was kind of like *The Gift of the Magi* with a perverse twist."

Conflicts over the house built up, and other tensions arose, too. Mary would come home at about six in the evening to a totally empty house (Richie was living with his father in Fresno). She'd study her script, sew new ribbons on her ballet slippers, try to find little things to keep her busy while she waited for Grant. By the time he got home, exhausted from a long day of business meetings, Grant was hungry for rest, Mary for companionship. Suddenly, arguments would arise for no reason. Shortly before Thanksgiving, they agreed to separate.

Grant moved into a rented cottage in the Hollywood Hills; Mary stayed at the new house in Malibu. The day Grant left, Mary was scheduled to appear at a press conference for British journalists. She refused to cancel it. Naturally, one of them inquired about her "marvelous marriage"—what was the secret of it? Mary managed to give the appropriately perky answer without the slightest sign of tears or tremor in her voice. Only her publicist, Dan Jenkins, knew just how impressive her performance was. He later told a *New York Times* writer, "I'll never forget that date. . . . Mary gave all the right answers, but when she got up to leave I could see her . . . kind of choking back a sob."

Mary kept a tight rein on her emotions at work, too. The cast and crew of *The Mary Tyler Moore Show* had no inkling of Mary's marital problems till that Friday night. It was the first time Grant Tinker was not in the control room watching the show being filmed. Ironically, that week's script dealt with Lou Grant leaving his wife after thirty years of marriage, and Mary helping him sell their house. When filming ended, producer Jim Brooks (one of the few people who knew her situation) embraced Mary as she was leaving the set, and she broke down and cried in his arms.

The next thing Mary and Grant knew there were rumors that she was dating Jim Brooks. Even though Mary and Grant had agreed not to communicate with each other for a while, those rumors forced a phone confrontation. Grant called Mary to assure her that he didn't believe the rumors and to suggest the best way to stop them. "Jim Brooks was a very dear friend to both of us," Mary later said. "It hurt Grant as much as it hurt me that Jim was being dragged into the middle of our problems."

By Christmas they both began to realize that the separation had been a mistake. It was the loneliest holiday either of them had ever spent. Mary went to Puerto Rico with friends, determined to have fun. Mostly she stayed in her hotel room and brooded. Grant spent Christmas in his Los Angeles apartment, never opening all the gifts from friends and family that were piled under his Christmas tree. Mary had given him an appointment book with a needlepoint cover that she'd done herself.

Right after New Year's, Grant sent Mary a note—ostensibly to discuss a few things about the show. The note led to a phone call, which in turn led to a dinner invitation. It was their first step toward reconciliation. They met after work in the studio parking lot and, before going out to dinner, Grant took Mary to his bachelor place, where they shared a drink. While Mary was there, Allen Ludden called. Allen and his wife, Betty White, were throwing a birthday dinner for Grant. On the spur of the moment Grant invited Mary to the dinner and she said yes. After that, they saw each other a few times a week—for dinner and the like—and by February 1974 they were back together on a full-time basis. In their mutual eagerness to make a new beginning of things, they decided to put the Malibu beach house up for sale and Mary moved into Grant's rented house until they could find a new place that suited them both.

Afterward, Mary assured magazine interviewers that her marriage was stronger because of the separation. During those two months apart, Grant and Mary had really faced themselves and their problems for the first time in a long time. They went back into the marriage knowing what was wrong and how to fix it.

But less than five years later, their relationship was in a shambles again. Her two abortive variety-show attempts definitely took a toll on the marriage. Professionally, in the two years since *The Mary Tyler Moore Show* had faded from the screen, Grant and Mary had grown farther and farther apart. MTM Enterprises was expanding into vistas that didn't include Mary as part of the talent package; and Mary herself was more anxious than ever to sink her teeth into a truly challenging role.

That opportunity came early in 1979, when Robert Redford sent her a script for a movie called *Ordinary People*. He wanted her to play the role of the mother, Beth Jarrett, a woman who keeps such a tight lid on her emotions that she finds it impossible to share her grief or comfort the rest of her family after her favorite son dies. Taking on that role would represent a definite turning point in Mary Tyler Moore's career as an actress. It would mark an end to what *People* magazine had once called Mary's inescapable image as "America's TV sweetheart. A vanilla madonna." Beth Jarrett was about as far away as you could get from Mary Richards and Laura Petrie.

By the time Mary got wind of the project, *Ordinary People* was already something of a publishing legend. The author, Judith Guest, was a Minneapolis housewife who had never written another piece of fiction before. She struggled over *Ordinary People* weekday mornings and afternoons while her children were at school, then sent the manuscript to several publishers in New York without any help from a literary agent. A young editor at Viking Press happened to get the unsolicited manuscript, and became Judith's advocate. In 1976, before the novel was even published, Robert Redford read a copy of the prepublication galleys and his brand-new production company, Wildwood Enterprises, purchased the screen rights. Redford seemed to have a natural instinct for sniffing out good film material. He had personally convinced Bob Woodward and Carl Bernstein to turn the story of their newspaper investigation of Watergate into a book; and after *All the President's Men* became a best-seller, Redford produced and starred in the film version.

He pictured Mary Tyler Moore as the mother the very first time he read *Ordinary People*, but he didn't move into action quickly. First Redford hired Alvin Sargent, the Oscar-winning screenwriter of *Julia*, to do the screenplay, and the two of them spent eighteen months working together until a script was finally completed. Then there were casting problems to iron out. Paramount Pictures, which was set to distribute the film, wanted Redford to play the father as well as direct, because Redford's face on screen would insure bigger box-office sales. Donald Sutherland, who eventually wound up playing the father, was originally supposed to portray the psychiatrist, Dr. Berger (a supporting role that ultimately went to Judd Hirsch). Actually, Redford's very first choice for the Berger role was Gene Hackman, who came close to signing a contract, but couldn't reach a financial agreement with Wildwood. (To keep costs down, because *Ordinary People* only had a $6 million budget, Redford himself only took a minimum salary as director—a little over $100,000 for twenty-six weeks' work.)

Ordinary People was a quiet film. Like *An Unmarried Woman, Coming Home,* and *Kramer vs. Kramer,* it focused on relationships that failed; in this case a family that completely fell apart after the accidental drowning of one son and the attempted suicide of the other. Calvin Jarrett, the father, was a well-to-do tax attorney in Lake Forest, Illinois; his wife, Beth, was the perfect homemaker and party hostess, but a woman totally unable to get in touch with her own feelings. Materially, the Jarretts were an enviable family, ensconced in their posh, well-manicured suburb; emotionally, they were trapped by an emptiness that threatened to engulf them all. In the end, only Conrad, the surviving son, learns to face the tragedy and move on with his life, through the help of a caring psychiatrist, Dr. Berger.

Robert Redford told *Playgirl* interviewer Merrill Shindler that he was attracted to *Ordinary People* because it "has a lot of colors. It's a picture about behavior, about something of depth. It has to do with the family unit, which interests me and . . . there are no villains in the piece. It concerns feelings people have but cannot handle because they cannot define them."

From the outset, Redford considered Beth the most interesting character in the piece because she was, on the one hand, the ultimate all-American girl, and on the other hand a lonely and pathetic creature. Beth's need for privacy— her determination not to let other people see her grief— was something Redford himself could identify with. As a Hollywood superstar, he constantly felt his privacy was invaded and tampered with. "I've gone through periods where I haven't been able to eat in a restaurant in peace. . . . Someday, I'd like to go back to living like a human being."

To some observers, *Ordinary People* seemed like a strange choice for Redford's maiden voyage as a film director. But Redford maintained that that's precisely why he chose to stake his reputation on it. "I wasn't interested in directing a film that had squealing tires and shoot-'em-up chases or that dealt with some indescribable force coming from outer space to eat us up," he explained. In *Ordinary People*, there were no commercial gimmicks at all, no dazzling special effects, no gratuitous doses of sex and violence. On screen it was simply a ninety-minute glimpse into one family's crisis, and whether you loved or hated the film depended entirely on how much you cared about the people in it.

Redford originally thought of Mary for the part of Beth because he had long been fascinated by what he called "the dark side of Mary Tyler Moore." He sensed it was always there, even in her portrayal of Mary Richards; this role would finally give her a chance to express it. "I've always felt that Mary Tyler Moore had dimensions which were not apparent in her television series," he informed the press. "She is more talented than people realize. And she embodies much of the American quality for me." *Newsweek* film critic Jack Kroll explained Redford's fascination with Mary's "dark side" in another way: "He saw something in TV's Mary Tyler Moore that nobody else saw—the tension behind that all-American smile."

According to Mary, it all began in early 1979, when she got her hands on a pirated script. After reading it, she decided she was absolutely perfect for the part of Beth Jarrett and told her agent to try and arrange a meeting with Robert Redford. Without realizing it, Mary was reading Redford's mind, because she was already a prime contender for the role, at least as far as he was concerned. At any rate, a luncheon meeting was set up where Mary and Redford met for the first time to discuss the possibility of her doing *Ordinary People*.

"Actually, Bob and I had known each other for years in a vague sort of way," Mary later recalled. "We used to pass each other on the beach at Malibu, but neither of us ever made the slightest effort to stop and say hello. We're both private kind of people—we didn't want to intrude on each other's thoughts."

At the luncheon meeting, Bob told Mary how much he had always admired her work—and she was equally complimentary. They talked in very general terms about *Ordinary People*—and Mary's feelings about the character of Beth—but nothing definite was decided. Redford told Mary that casting was still very much up in the air and promised to get back to her. She walked out of his office and didn't hear from him for two months.

During that time Mary became desperate with anticipation, but tried not to show it. She heard through the Hollywood grapevine that Redford was testing practically every forty-year-old actress around. At one point, according to newspaper columnists, Lee Remick was supposed to be the leading contender for the role. That rumor, coupled with the fact that Redford hadn't communicated with her at all, made Mary feel almost certain that she'd been eliminated from the running.

"It was truly a nerve-wracking time for me," she recalls.

"I hadn't felt like this since I was twenty-three and auditioning for *The Dick Van Dyke Show*."

When Redford finally called, the conversation didn't calm Mary's anxieties in the least. He simply wanted her to know that he hadn't lost interest in her, but he was still trying to solve other casting problems. His chief dilemma seemed to be the choice of a leading man. Obviously, Paramount was still pushing for Redford to take that role himself. Mary thanked him for calling to keep her up to date on the situation and assured him that she understood entirely. Actually, she was growing more and more anxious as each day passed—and still no word on Beth Jarrett.

Nearly three months after their first meeting, Redford was finally ready to cast Beth—and he asked Mary and Donald Sutherland to meet in his office. In a strange way, Redford's procrastination had turned out to be an unexpected plus for Mary. During that waiting period, her second TV variety series had failed, clearing her work schedule completely. "It just goes to show what a good thing failure sometimes is," says Mary. "If I'd still been doing my variety show, I probably would have had to turn down *Ordinary People*, no matter how badly I wanted the role, because of a time conflict."

Mary looked forward to her first meeting with Donald Sutherland in a state of total panic. She realized that everything depended on it. She would only get to play Beth—the part of a lifetime—if Redford felt that she and Sutherland had the right chemistry. As Mary later described the scene to writer Michael Ver Meulen, "I thought, 'Oh, my God, this is going to be the toughest thing in my life, because I know that he is going to be looking at me with a magnifying glass. . . .'"

Sitting in Redford's office, Mary felt totally helpless. Sutherland was polite, but reserved. Redford made small talk about baseball, and *Ordinary People* was only referred to in general terms—neither of the actors present wanted to seem too eager for the role. While everybody chatted, a hairdresser and costume designer came in to discuss the right "look" for Beth in the movie, but Mary still wasn't sure the part was hers. Redford had never come out and offered it to her point-blank. Maybe he was doing the same thing with Lee Remick and who knows how many other actresses, thought Mary as she left.

But the torture was nearly over. Later that afternoon, while sitting in her manager's office, Mary learned that Redford had called to negotiate a contract. Donald Sutherland would indeed be playing her husband, and Mary would get billing right after him. That fact didn't bother her at all. As she later told *New York Times* reporter Judy Klemesrud, "I couldn't care less about billing. It does nothing for my ego. For me, it's the work. Besides, Donald is a motion-picture actor. I have some celebrity from television, but he has the biggest part."

After signing the contract, the first thing Mary did was show the film script to her psychiatrist. A key theme hinged on Beth's inability to show any feeling or affection for her son Conrad (played by Timothy Hutton)—when Conrad slashes his wrists, Beth's first thought is that he messed up the bathroom and she'll have to get the tile regrouted—and Mary found it difficult to identify with Beth as a mother. She wanted to know if a mother could indeed be that alienated from a child; her doctor assured her such a reaction was indeed valid and he helped her find the right sense of motivation. (Interestingly enough, although Mary's relationship with her own son, Richie, was a troubled one, she saw no parallels between Beth and herself as mothers. In only one scene—a brief moment of affection between Beth and Conrad—did Mary admit to drawing from memories of her own experiences with Richie to bring tears to her eyes.)

Not that Mary didn't see anything of herself in Beth. "Beth has a strength of purpose, a determination. So do I," she said. "She has a respect for organization and a certain optimism and I do, too." Like Beth, Mary kept a tight rein on her feelings at all times, rarely revealed her true emotions in public, and made friends slowly. The perfectionist aspects of Beth's character were all deeply ingrained in Mary's psyche, too.

But beyond their mutual take-charge, no-nonsense approach to life, Beth and Mary parted company. Beth would never seek psychiatric help; Mary has been through years of analysis. Moreover, Beth derives much of her identity from her success as a homemaker. She's a compulsive cleaner, a terrific cook, a successful hostess. Mary laughingly admits she falls totally apart in all those areas and couldn't survive a single day without household help to bail her out in the kitchen. Most importantly, Beth's strength and self-sufficiency turns out to be an illusion. "She lives in her own highly controlled world, and when that is shattered she refuses to accept help," says Mary. "So her strength becomes her weakness. I'm not like that. But I've seen that feeling in friends and members of my own family, and I can make their reactions my own in the film."

In doing *Ordinary People*, Mary and Redford were each taking an equal gamble on the other. He had never directed a film before; she had never undertaken such a complex, multitextured role. But they couldn't have been more in sync with each other if they'd been collaborating for ten years. Actually, they were the same age—Bob was born on August 18, 1937, just four months before Mary—and he was also a product of Southern California culture (raised in Los Angeles, just as Mary had been).

Their rapport on the set was instantaneous. Although Mary admitted she couldn't help simply admiring Redford's good looks—in one magazine interview she compared his face to that of Michelangelo's *David*—she soon realized he was more than just another pretty face. She was charmed by his intelligence and the ease with which he took control on the set.

Mary didn't realize that Redford's bravado, especially when filming began, was just a sham. "I had to give one of the best performances of my life," he later confided. "I had to walk around the set like I knew what I was doing! If I wasn't certain what to do next, I'd just look very thoughtful and authoritative. In other words, I faked it!"

Filming commenced on October 9, 1979, and most of it was done on location in Lake Forest, Illinois, and other surrounding Chicago suburbs. And if Redford was quaking in his boots, the rest of the cast certainly wasn't aware of it, at least not Mary. She told the *Chicago Tribune*'s associate editor, Clifford Terry, that "Bob's the best director I've ever worked with. He's phenomenally talented and handles all the problems as if this were his twenty-fifth film. . . . He's as kind and considerate to the man who sweeps the cigarettes off the floor as he is to the principals. He has a wonderful sense of humor and *I love him madly.*"

Yet it wasn't all roses and lollipops. By Redford's own admission, there were days when he wanted "to go off and smash something." Mary's TV mannerisms—the way she'd cock her head or shrug her shoulders—were too reminiscent of her former incarnation as Mary Richards, and they really troubled Redford at first. But he managed to get Mary to leave the last vestiges of her TV shtick behind without ruffling her sensitive feathers. In the end he helped her tap emotional depths within herself that Mary had never allowed to surface on screen before, and, by showing the dark side of Mary Tyler Moore, helped her create a character who was both human and unforgettable.

As an actor himself, Redford was aware that dialogue and blocking have to be kept fluid or performances tend to petrify. He let the cast improvise and make changes in scenes at will as long as they kept to the broad strokes of the script and didn't change the point of any scene. Mary particularly thrived under that kind of liberated atmosphere because it was so similar to her working experience on both her own show and *Dick Van Dyke.*

During their stay in Lake Forest, Mary, Donald Sutherland, and Robert Redford all rented private houses, while the rest of the cast and crew lived in a motel in nearby Waukegan. For the interior scenes, Redford borrowed an unused laundry building and created a $200,000 reproduction (fourteen rooms in all) of a Lake Forest house. For the exterior shots, many local landmarks were temporarily taken over. There were scenes of Mary shopping in a real K-Mart, of her playing tennis at the Waukegan Tennis Club, and of Timothy Hutton and Dinah Manoff sitting at a soda fountain in Skokie.

Neiman-Marcus turned over their fur salon to Redford and company for a morning's worth of shooting, but the cast and crew had to be assembled before dawn. Shooting began at six A.M., so that all the lights and equipment could be removed by ten A.M. when the fur salon actually opened for business.

While Mary simply browsed around town in her spare time, soaking up Lake Forest culture, Timothy Hutton spent a week touring mental hospitals in the area and mingling with patients. In the script, his character, Conrad, had just been released from a mental hospital, following his suicide attempt, and Timothy wanted to get as much background as possible for the role. During his tours, he never mentioned that he was making a movie, nor even that he was really an actor. The inmates he spoke with simply assumed that he was a reasonably recovered outpatient.

During their two-month stay in Lake Forest, the *Ordinary People* company were obviously the center of attention. On the first day of shooting, Robert Redford's director chair was stolen (presumably by an eager souvenir-hunter); later on, Redford's sunglasses were pilfered, too. Local residents fell over each other trying to establish personal contact with the visiting celebrities. Redford got over one hundred invitations to dinner at private homes of people he'd never met; Mary Tyler Moore ran a close second. The cast was also bombarded with requests to christen new supermarkets, give Brownie troops a guided tour of the set, and donate their personal clothing to various charity auctions. Redford did agree to march in the Lake Forest High School Homecoming Parade, but he had an ulterior motive. While Redford rode on top of a flower-strewn float, smiling and waving to the crowds, his hidden cameras were photographing groups of townspeople to use as insert shots in *Ordinary People.*

While residents competed with each other in collecting cast autographs, actually landing a day's work in the film became a real mark of distinction. Some of the town's wealthiest matrons would send the casting director and his staff homemade pies and cakes each week, hoping they could bribe their way into a walk-on role. When a single call for extras was broadcast on the local radio station, the response was phenomenal. In one day, 892 women, 42 men, and 1 Airedale showed up, hoping for a part.

For Redford, being on location was a tough race against time. He wanted to be back in Hollywood, ready to edit the film, before Chicago's blizzard weather set in in January and February. For Mary, there was an added burden. She had gone to Lake Forest knowing that her seventeen-year marriage to Grant Tinker was pretty much unsalvageable, and in the midst of filming a formal announcement of their separation was released to the press.

After finishing *Ordinary People*, Mary wouldn't be returning to California at all. On January 20, 1980, she was due in New York to begin rehearsals of *Whose Life Is It, Anyway?*, which would mark her dramatic debut on Broadway. It would also be her first return to the Great White Way after her stinging defeat there in *Breakfast at Tiffany's* thirteen years before.

Mary didn't know it yet, but both projects—*Ordinary People* and *Whose Life Is It, Anyway?*—were destined to bring her the greatest professional acclaim of her life. When *Ordinary People* premiered in mid-1980, Vincent Canby of *The New York Times* wrote that "Miss Moore is remarkably fine, simultaneously delicate and tough and desperate." In his *New York Post* review, Stephen M. Silverman noted that "the surprise of the movie is Mary Tyler Moore as the cold as enamel mother, Beth, revealing that indeed, there is a flip side to MTM, Mary Richards, and Laura Petrie—in fact, all her TV personas."

As 1980 dawned and Mary made plans to move quietly back to New York once again, she had no idea that the most stunning—and heartbreaking—year of her life was about to begin. Before the year was out, she would garner a Tony —Broadway's highest accolade—march toward an Academy Award nomination, and then suffer the cruelest kind of devastation a human being can ever know.

❧ 9 ❧

The Elephant Woman?

"No part will be safe if Mary Tyler Moore's amendment goes through," Gardner McKay, the theater critic for the *Los Angeles Herald Examiner*, wrote in September 1979. What exactly was the "Mary Tyler Moore amendment" (as McKay so acidly put it)? It was the announcement that Mary Tyler Moore—a woman and a mere television performer (*Ordinary People* hadn't been made, let alone released yet)—would replace Tom Conti—an award-winning stage actor—in the Broadway production of *Whose Life Is It, Anyway?*

What was so threatening about this prospect? Well, according to critics like McKay, if the lead character in *Whose Life Is It, Anyway?* could undergo a sex switch, then we had better brace ourselves for such mangled masterpieces as "*Hamlet, Princess of Denmark,*" "*The Elephant Woman,*" and "*Death of a Salesperson.*" Beneath the sarcasm, the message was clear: Mary Tyler Moore's forthcoming dramatic debut at the Royale Theatre in New York might have a certain shock value, but few critics were prepared to take her performance seriously.

In 1979, *Tootsie* and *Victor/Victoria* were still a few years off; and while it might be okay for men and women to wear the same jeans, slipping into each other's roles was a different matter entirely. True, Mary would be portraying a female character, not impersonating one, but to many Broadway savants there was still something gimmicky about the whole business.

Practically everyone expected Mary to fail, just as she had thirteen years before in *Breakfast at Tiffany's*. *Whose Life* was the kind of extraordinary challenge that might defeat even the most seasoned theater veteran, and Mary—for all her fame and popularity in television—was hardly that.

She was leaping head first (or rather heart first, head second) into a project that would test all her nerve and endurance. *Whose Life Is It, Anyway?* was the compelling story of a quadriplegic who battles every medical, legal, and moral obstacle to win the right to die. As Ken Harrison —the embittered hero who prefers quick termination to a prolonged living death—Tom Conti had won a Tony Award and would have been a hard act for any actor to follow. In addition, some observers felt that the maleness of the character was so deeply rooted in the story and dialogue that the sex transformation simply wouldn't work.

Not everybody was against the experiment, though. Some critics thought Mary doing *Whose Life* just might be the coup of the theater season. After all, hadn't Pearl Bailey successfully replaced Carol Channing in *Hello, Dolly*, even though Dolly Gallagher Levi was supposed to be as Irish as soda bread? And there were other precedents, too. Sarah Bernhardt and Judith Anderson had both played *Hamlet;* and Peter Pan—a distinctly boyish character—had always been portrayed on stage by a woman.

The idea of turning Ken into Claire had first been suggested by actress Jane Asher in 1978. At the time, she was playing the hero's sympathetic physician in the original London production of *Whose Life Is It, Anyway?* and she

thought it might be a marvelous change of pace if she and
Tom Conti switched roles as doctor and patient for a while.
Sex aside, role-swapping is hardly an unheard-of theater
custom. In many Shakespearean companies, the actors
playing Othello and Iago often trade roles; and Laurence
Olivier played first the martyred saint, then Henry II, in
the 1960 production of *Becket*. Art Carney and Walter Matthau had talked about switching off as Felix and Oscar
when they co-starred in *The Odd Couple*.

Brian Clark, the author of *Whose Life*, was intrigued by
Jane Asher's suggestion, but never had a chance to follow
it up. Tom Conti was already packing to bring *Whose Life*
to New York (with Jean Marsh taking over Jane Asher's
role). A replacement for Conti in the London production
had to be found quickly. There was no time for Clark to
rewrite the entire play and then remount it with Jane
Asher in the leading role.

In New York, producer Manny Azenberg and director
Michael Lindsay-Hogg kept mentioning the sex-switch
idea to friends, but were met with constant disapproval.
According to Lindsay-Hogg, "Everyone we approached
turned purple at the idea of a female quadriplegic on stage.
They couldn't see her opting for the right to die the way
a man would. I found that kind of reasoning terribly nar-
row-minded. It only made me more adamant to do it."

When Tom Conti dropped out of the New York run,
finding a suitable replacement for him became a mammoth
task. Some stars wanted too much money; others were
afraid of being measured against Conti's award-winning
performance. Among the name actors who turned down
the lead in *Whose Life*, for one reason or another, were Jon
Voight, Jim Dale, Dustin Hoffman, Richard Dreyfuss (who
later did the film version), Anthony Hopkins, and Al
Pacino. One of the turn-downs, Richard Thomas, just hap-

pened to have the same agent as Mary Tyler Moore, which is how she came to hear of the project.

At this point in 1979, *Ordinary People* was still up in the air and Mary told her agent to be on the alert for possible theater roles for her. A week after she gave him those instructions, Azenberg called to inquire about the availability of Richard Thomas. When that didn't pan out, he casually mentioned that if he couldn't find a name actor soon, he just might put a woman in the role. Mary's agent immediately said, "Well, how about Mary Tyler Moore?"

But even once the decision was made to transform Ken Harrison into Claire, Mary wasn't on the A list of contenders. Meryl Streep, the first actress asked, had to bow out because of pregnancy; Marsha Mason was unavailable because of film commitments.

Meanwhile, Mary herself wasn't too sure she wanted to take the risk. She had never seen the play, and had no particular fascination with the lead character. Mary, a survivor, found it difficult to relate to a character, male or female, who so desperately wanted to die. Mary flew to New York with Grant Tinker and they sat through two performances of *Whose Life* in one day. "We were riveted both times," she later said. By the time they left the theater that night, Mary had no doubts at all—she believed *Whose Life Is It, Anyway?* was a masterpiece and Claire Harrison the role of a lifetime.

Moving to New York posed no problem, either; in fact, it would give Mary a real chance to "start over" now that there seemed little hope of saving her marriage. Grant and Mary were still friendly enough for him to be involved in her negotiations for both *Ordinary People* and *Whose Life*, but the only bond between them was professional now. In September 1979, when Manny Azenberg announced that

Mary would replace Tom Conti in *Whose Life*, she was already committed to begin filming *Ordinary People* a month later. Tom Conti had to be out of the show by the end of October because he was slated to direct a new Frank Gilroy play, *Last Licks*, which was due to open November 20 at the Longacre Theatre. So Azenberg decided to close down *Whose Life* after Tom Conti left and wait till the following February to reopen it with Mary. That would give her enough time to finish *Ordinary People*, while playwright Brian Clark revamped *Whose Life* and turned his protagonist into a woman.

In reality, it only took Brian Clark three weeks to make the necessary changes. On January 20, 1980, Mary began rehearsals, with James Naughton playing the doctor. Tom Conti spent ten days with her, helping Mary master some of the physical demands of the role. As a quadriplegic, she wouldn't even be able to move a muscle on stage, let alone scratch an itch. The entire performance would be in her voice, her eyes, her face. Mary would have to be in total control of her body at all times. Conti urged her to lie on two pillows, not one, so she wouldn't get sore by the end of each performance.

Mary actually began learning the part at home long before rehearsals began. Every night she would lie awake in bed, before going to sleep, waiting for restlessness to set in and trying to control the urge to twitch or scratch an itch. But Mary had no trouble learning to fall into a state of complete motionlessness. As she told *New York Times* writer Janet Maslin, "I think one of the things that stood me in very good stead is the fact that I am a dancer and, from that training, I know how to isolate parts of my body. That's allowed me to make the adjustment to keeping absolutely stock still."

In preparation, Mary also read several biographies of quadriplegics and visited a Los Angeles hospital for the disabled where she talked to patients about their disabilities, hopes, and frustrations. Mary worried (needlessly, as it turned out) that her voice wouldn't carry in the theater, but she had no trouble relating to Claire Harrison once rehearsals began. As a diabetic, Mary found it easy to understand Claire's impatience with her malfunctioning body, to identify with Claire's anger at the stupidity of fate.

On February 24, 1980, Mary braved the critics and opened on Broadway in *Whose Life Is It, Anyway?* Of all the telegrams she got, Ed Asner's was perhaps the funniest and most affectionate: "Nice to know all those dancing lessons have paid off at last," he wired her. The next morning the New York newspapers had equally loving comments. Walter Kerr of *The New York Times* declared that Mary's performance was "accomplished and finally quite moving." A few days later, T. E. Kalem of *Time* magazine wrote: "As for Mary Tyler Moore, she has tackled the play with aplomb. Her eyes are pools of pain across which imps of mischief sail. Her charm could heat igloos. Without taking a single step, she has made the transition from TV to the stage in perfect stride."

There were only a few clouds ruffling her horizon. One critic, John Simon, wrote that he couldn't understand why Claire would want to terminate her life because, as a quadriplegic, her sex life was over. He could understand a man feeling that way, but not a woman. Mary was furious over that—it irked her that such blatant chauvinism could pass for theater criticism. But the hosannahs far overshadowed the few sour notes. Carol Burnett lauded Mary's courage in tackling the role. "I admire Mary so much," she said. "If someone asked me to do that, I'd say, 'Sure, I'll do it—in Hungary, where no one would see me!'"

Robert Redford, her *Ordinary People* mentor, was equally complimentary. After the show, he came backstage to congratulate Mary and told her, "I'm proud of you—I feel like your father!" And columnists in the Hollywood trade papers began hypothesizing that Mary just might get the film version of *Whose Life*, even though Redford himself was supposedly interested in doing the role on screen.

Despite all the accolades, though, Mary's success didn't translate into instant box-office sales. On March 5, 1980, *Variety* noted that *Whose Life* was suffering from a "slow start at the box office" even though "it's generally agreed in the trade that her portrayal is emotionally involving and exceptionally accomplished." A Hollywood name on the marquee seemed to be no guarantee of ticket sales. Richard Gere in *Bent*, Mia Farrow in *Romantic Comedy*, and Roy Scheider in *Betrayal* didn't turn those shows into blockbuster hits, although Sandy Duncan's *Peter Pan* and Mickey Rooney's *Sugar Babies* were both bona fide successes.

During her three-month run in the play, Mary experienced the ultimate highs and lows of being a New York theater actor. At the same time that she was receiving anonymous death threats in the mail, she was getting standing ovations on stage every night. When it came time for the annual Tony nominations, Mary looked like a leading best-actress contender, but she was declared ineligible on a technicality (she had replaced another actor in the role). Instead, the award went to Phyllis Frelich, a nonspeaking, nonhearing actress who was turning in a brilliant performance in another Manny Azenberg production, *Children of a Lesser God*.

But Mary wasn't overlooked on Tony night—she received a special award in recognition of her contribution to the theater that season—and the whole evening was something of a glorious reunion for her. Judd Hirsch, one of her

Ordinary People co-stars, was a best-actor nominee for *Talley's Folly* (he lost to *Children of a Lesser God*'s John Rubinstein) and Dinah Manoff, who'd played a small role in *Ordinary People,* won a best-supporting-actress Tony for Neil Simon's *I Ought to Be in Pictures.*

With the end of *Whose Life Is It, Anyway?,* and the successful premiere of *Ordinary People,* Mary decided to live in New York permanently. She told *New York Times* interviewer Judy Klemesrud that "Los Angeles is great when you're married and lying out by the pool with a dog." In New York, Mary could go to parties alone and not feel like a fifth wheel. People weren't categorized as couples. Moreover, her whole life was different since her last stay in New York in the mid-1960s. Then, her son Richie was only ten years old; now he was living in Los Angeles on his own. Without the presence of a husband or a son, Mary suddenly had a mobility and freedom that she had never really experienced before. She had spent all of her adult life being married; she was finally starting to live out the theme song from her old situation-comedy show, finally starting to *make it on her own.*

Through it all, Grant and Mary remained friendly. They had no immediate plans to divorce, since, as Mary put it, "we like each other too much to contemplate anything so final and unfriendly." In September Mary was contemplating a trip to France with her friend, actress Pippa Scott— they wanted to go ballooning together—and she was also expanding her political horizons. Although Mary was a lifelong Republican, she decided—perhaps as another act of independence—to support Jimmy Carter's reelection, and even filmed a campaign commercial for him.

Mary didn't know what her next project would be, but she was definitely ruling out a comedy or a musical. As a dramatic actress, she was on a winning streak, what with three bona fide triumphs in a row (*First, You Cry, Whose Life,* and *Ordinary People*), and she wanted to find another film or play that explored relationships. In January of 1980, she had already turned down a lucrative chance to co-star with Dick Van Dyke in a cable-TV presentation of the musical *I Do, I Do.* The idea was to bring Dick and Mary together while they were both in New York (she doing *Whose Life,* he starring in the revival of *The Music Man*).

Even though her separation from Grant Tinker remained amicable and civilized, Mary was starting to get on with her personal life, too. In March, she began dating Michael Lindsay-Hogg, her *Whose Life Is It, Anyway?* director, although Mary maintained that she was still too new at being a bachelor girl to feel free about discussing her romantic life with the press.

By October it was clear that *Ordinary People* had become one of the major films of the year and stood a good chance of winning an Academy Award. Mary seemed an obvious choice for a nomination, too. Her chief competitors were Sissy Spacek (*Coal Miner's Daughter*) and Goldie Hawn (*Private Benjamin*).

Mary would definitely return to Los Angeles for the Oscar ceremonies and for the endless rounds of promotion that are part and parcel of being a contender. It showed every sign of being a truly triumphant return. Mary, the queen of television, had now conquered Broadway and motion pictures, too.

But even Mary couldn't have guessed just how soon she'd be back in Hollywood. It wasn't Oscars or Golden Apples that brought her back. It was the death of her only son.

❧ 10 ❧

Loss

All her life Mary Tyler Moore had hated guns. One of the things that bothered her most about her first husband, Richard Meeker, was his fascination with hunting. And she was even more troubled that her son, Richie, felt the same way his father did. In a 1976 interview in *Good Housekeeping*, Mary was very vocal about the fact that neither her ex-husband nor her son would take her seriously on the subject. "The frustrating thing for me is that my son really does love animals," said Mary. "Find a bird with a broken wing or an injured squirrel and he is there to mend it and nurse it. I'll never understand how Richie can just turn off those feelings when he discusses hunting."

Killing animals wasn't the only thing that Mary and Richie didn't see eye to eye on. A few weeks after Richie's death in 1980, the *National Enquirer* declared unequivocally: "Mary Tyler Moore was too busy being America's sweetheart to be a mother to her only son Richard—and give him the love he desperately craved." The article went on to allege that Mary had been so consumed by professional ambition for so many years that she never had time to nurture a real relationship with Richie. According to the *Enquirer*, Richie for a time became "a dropout" and "a drifter" before he accidentally shot himself to death on October 14, 1980.

Yet no one would deny that Mary loved her son deeply. Was it coincidence that Laura Petrie's son on *The Dick Van Dyke Show* was named Richie? Or that Mary chose *Richards* as her character's last name on *The Mary Tyler Moore Show?* Probably not. Although she may have been an absentee parent much of the time, Mary was trying very hard to send Richie signals that he was still important in her life.

Richie's parents were divorced when he was six. He barely had time to adjust to that change when Mary married Grant Tinker—and Richie had to learn to deal with a stepfather and occasional visits from four stepsiblings. As a teenager, Richie saw that Grant and Mary's strongest attachments were to their careers. He was often lonely and left to his own devices. Finally, at the age of seventeen, he moved to Fresno to live with his father, Richard Meeker, and his stepmother, Jeanette.

By Mary's own admission, Richie's teenage years were a period of extreme alienation from her. "He rebelled against my affluence," she said. But it wasn't only the Tinkers' Bel Air lifestyle that Richie found so stifling and barren; it was Mary's rigidity, combined with her total absorption in herself and in her career. Richie was going through the rigors of adolescence just when *The Mary Tyler Moore Show* was at the zenith. She was working long days, every day, striving for perfection on her show, more at home, in a sense, in her dressing room than in the home she shared with Grant and Richie. Mary's hold on personal relationships was tenuous, indeed. Around the same time that Richie opted to live with his father, Grant and Mary's first trial separation occurred.

When Richie's father—a TV station manager—was

transferred from Fresno to Sacramento, Richie chose to
stay on his own for a while. Reportedly he even spent a
night sleeping on a park bench in Fresno. According to
People magazine, Richie was popular at Bullard High,
where he "was looked up to as a natural athlete and a free
spirit." He occasionally returned to Los Angeles, but the
friction with his mother remained intense. Mary wasn't
happy with his school grades (shades of her father's own
attitude toward her), his choice of girlfriends, or his use of
marijuana. Sometimes her battles with Richie even became
public. Mary rarely lost her temper at work, but when
Richie showed up sporting a large and ugly tattoo of a
dragon on his arm, Mary chewed him out within earshot
of the whole *MTM* cast and crew.

After graduation, Richie returned to Los Angeles and
lived on his own. He worked in the loan department of a
bank and for two and a half years lived with a young
woman named Kelly Wilson. Kelly later remembered him
as "well-adjusted" and "normal . . . just a big kid who never
really wanted to grow up." During this time, mother and
son began to mend their differences. In fact, after Richie's
death, Mary's New York press agent, Paula Green, admitted that Mary and Richie "went through a period when
they didn't get along too well. But that all ended this year
and they became really close." Paula Green also maintained that Mary and Richie spoke on the phone to each
other at least twice a week, and that he had called Mary and
had a very pleasant conversation with her a few hours
before he died.

During the last year of his life, Richie suddenly expressed interest in becoming an actor—something that had
never tempted him before. While he worked in the mail
room at CBS, he auditioned for a part on *The Young and the
Restless* (which he didn't get) and a part on *Dukes of Hazzard*

(which he did). Unfortunately, the television actors' strike, which hit Los Angeles in the summer and fall of 1980, closed down all production, and Richie never got a chance to actually do his *Dukes of Hazzard* stint.

He refused to let his mother or his stepfather, Grant Tinker, pave the way for him, and was determined to make it on his own. According to Paula Green, Richie's sense of confidence about his acting career was the main topic of discussion during his last phone call to his mother. They talked happily about her success on Broadway and Richie's feelings that he was finally beginning to get somewhere in Hollywood.

A very public sign that Richie was drawing closer to his mother came in the summer of 1980 when he accompanied her to a private screening of *Ordinary People*. It corroborated what Mary had been telling the press for some time—that she and her only son were finally beginning to come to terms with each other. Early in 1980, Mary had told the *Star:* "We went through a fairly long period of not communicating. He had, I think, some resentments of my commitment to my work. He's beginning to understand that I was doing the best that I could at the time. . . . It's nice, I have a new friend."

That summer Richie also changed his living arrangements once again. He moved into a small house in central Los Angeles with two friends, Janet McLaughlin and Judy Vasquez. His relationship with both girls was strictly platonic. Janet, twenty-two, was an old friend of his from Fresno; and Judy was, in turn, a friend of Janet's. The house was located on a quiet street near the University of Southern California, where Janet was a student.

In May, Janet had been burglarized while she was sleeping, and because of that Richie kept a .410-gauge shotgun in the house. It hung on a bedroom wall. On the night of

October 14, Richie was apparently in good spirits. Early in the evening, he talked with Janet McLaughlin about his plans for fixing up the house; he massaged a cramp in her foot and put up some bookshelves for her. Then, while Janet went off to her bedroom to study, Richie phoned his mom and Linda Jason, a girlfriend of his in Fresno.

Judy Vasquez, a student at Cal State, came home at about ten-thirty P.M. He had just finished talking with Linda Jason and reportedly was in a playful mood. While he sat on his bed, talking with Judy, he suddenly took his shotgun down from the wall and began playing with it. According to Judy Vasquez (as reported in the *Star*), "He was loading it and unloading it, saying, 'She loves me, she loves me not,' with the barrel of the gun facing him." Judy begged him to put the gun down. Richie replied, "I know what I'm doing"—then, a few moments later, the gun went off, killing him.

"Judy screamed and I ran out," Janet McLaughlin later told the *Los Angeles Times*. "She screamed that Richard had been shot." At first, Janet thought that an intruder had shot Richie; then she realized that Richie had pulled the trigger himself. Both girls ran to neighbors for help. Art Curtis, a painter who lived directly across the street, called the police and an ambulance when he found Judy Vasquez screaming and hysterical on his doorstep. She was crying, "Oh God, he shot himself. This is a fantasy. It's not happening!"

Richie was taken to Western Park Hospital. According to the *Los Angeles Times*, he died shortly before midnight "of a shotgun blast to the face." Janet McLaughlin called Grant Tinker who, in turn, called Mary in New York. Richie's father was notified soon afterward.

After an investigation by the coroner's office, the official verdict was that Richard Meeker, Jr., had died as the result

of an accidental, self-inflicted bullet wound. There was still
much confusion about what had actually happened, since
press reports tended to differ. According to some newspaper stories, Richie had been playing "shotgun roulette,"
but in *People* Janet McLaughlin disputed that. She said she
didn't know how the gun had gone off, but it had no safety
catch and had malfunctioned a few weeks earlier.

Everyone close to the family maintained that Richie
certainly hadn't been despondent over anything. The
weekend before his death he had gone to Fresno to visit
Linda Jason. According to her mother, he had acted as if
he was "feeling on top of the world." His stepmother,
Jeanette Meeker, reiterated that Richie seemed "happy
and contented" during her last phone conversation with
him, too.

The funeral was especially traumatic for Mary. She wept
all through the service. All of her former TV colleagues
rallied around her, and Edward Asner was particularly
supportive. "He just held me in his arms and sobbed half
the night through with me," she said. Dick Van Dyke sent
flowers and phoned Mary at least twice each day to see how
she was doing. Other messages of support and sympathy
flowed in, too. President Carter phoned her three times and
the Rev. Billy Graham called twice. Oral Roberts, Sammy
Davis, Jr., and Frank Sinatra sent their personal condo-
lences as well.

Mary leaned on both her psychiatrist and her medical
doctor through this crisis—and her business associates, too.
She told her office staff, "I just don't know how I ever
would have made it through this tragedy without your
help."

After the funeral, Richie's body was cremated and his
ashes were scattered in the Owens River, in a beautiful part
of the Sierras that Richie had particularly loved. Mary and

Grant were joined only by Richard and Jeanette Meeker for this final, and very private, rite.

While Mary was trying her best to recover from this tragedy, she and Grant grew closer again. They even made one last attempt to salvage their marriage, but this reconciliation barely lasted a month. On December 30, 1980, Mary took the first legal steps toward formally dissolving their marriage. She filed suit for divorce in Los Angeles Superior Court, citing irreconcilable differences as grounds for ending the union. Mary waived alimony and listed September 30 as the formal date of separation (in other words, denying the brief reconciliation which had taken place after Richie's death).

Although she mourned privately, Mary made no effort to cut down on her public visibility. Just a few days after Richie's funeral, she kept a luncheon appointment to discuss possible film projects. She seemed insistent on pursuing her professional and social life with a vengeance, as if keeping busy was the only way she could cope with bereavement. In November, she had a two-and-a-half-hour lunch with Robert Redford at La Pomme, on New York's East Side. A few days later, she dined with Warren Beatty at Serendipity, a restaurant just around the corner from her apartment.

Only two months after Richie's death, Mary was being seen all over Manhattan, beautifully dressed and coiffed, the perfect picture of elegance. She refused to let even this tragedy defeat her. "Pain," Mary had once said, "nourishes my courage. You have to fail in order to practice being brave. You can't be brave if you've had only wonderful things happen to you."

In December, at the same time that Mary was filing for divorce, *Ordinary People* was voted best picture of the year by the New York Film Critics Circle, a good indication that it might win an Oscar next spring. Suddenly the film had become a morbid echo of Mary's own life, and it seemed bitterly ironic that Mary might now win an Academy Award for playing a mother trying to cope with the death of a beloved son.

Despite her own situation, Mary put her all into helping promote *Ordinary People* in the Oscar race, and she was especially hopeful that her mentor, Robert Redford, would be picked as best director. But when the fifty-third annual Academy Awards telecast rolled around, all the usual hype and hoopla had to take a back seat to a far more pressing news event: John Hinckley's attempt to assassinate President Reagan. The awards had to be postponed one day— from March 30 to March 31, 1981—because the networks were devoting practically round-the-clock news coverage to the President's condition.

The awards themselves were a pretty routine affair. It wasn't one of those suspenseful years when several big movies were battling it out for the big prize—and none of the nominees were threatening to show up pregnant and unmarried (as Vanessa Redgrave once did) or promising not to accept the Oscar if they won (à la George C. Scott).

In the best-picture race, *Ordinary People* didn't have much competition. None of the other four nominees—*Coal Miner's Daughter*, *The Elephant Man*, *Raging Bull*, and *Tess*— seemed likely to cause an upset. Most of the other categories held no surprises either. Long before the envelopes were opened, it was a foregone conclusion that Robert De Niro would be named best actor for his performance in *Raging Bull* and that *Ordinary People* would take the lion's share of the prizes, including best supporting actor (Timothy Hutton), best director (Redford), and best screenplay adaptation (Alvin Sargent). In the best supporting actress

contest, *Melvin and Howard*'s Mary Steenburgen was also
considered a shoo-in.

There was a small ripple of excitement when Dolly Par-
ton's "9 to 5" and Willie Nelson's "On the Road Again"
were both passed over as song of the year in favor of the
title song from *Fame,* but only one race—best actress—was
really too close to call. There wasn't a single lightweight
contender on the list. Each of the five nominated actresses
—Mary Tyler Moore (*Ordinary People*), Ellen Burstyn (*Resurrection*), Goldie Hawn (*Private Benjamin*), Gena Rowlands
(*Gloria*), and Sissy Spacek (*Coal Miner's Daughter*)—had
given, it could be argued, the most intriguing performance
of her career. All of them deserved to win; obviously, only
one lady would.

Granted, Ellen Burstyn and Gena Rowlands were both
long shots, since their films—*Resurrection* and *Gloria*—were
the kind of masterpieces that the critics loved, but the public hadn't flocked to in droves. Besides, Ellen already had
an Oscar (for *Alice Doesn't Live Here Anymore*) and Gena's
film appearances were so few and far between that Hollywood hardly thought of her as a screen actress at all. But
Goldie Hawn was another story. Her zany comedy, *Private
Benjamin,* had turned out to be one of the year's biggest
money-makers—and *Coal Miner's Daughter* was also a huge
success. Sissy Spacek—best known as the deranged teenager in *Carrie*—had done a complete image switch in the
screen biography of country-western star Loretta Lynn.
And Sissy got extra points from Oscar voters for doing all
her own singing in the movie.

In *Ordinary People* Mary Tyler Moore had also radically
altered her screen image, but perhaps not in the right direction as far as Oscar was concerned. Her portrayal of Beth
Jarrett—a cold, stern, unapproachable woman, totally

alienated from her family, unable to feel anything, not even grief over a son's death—was hardly the kind of characterization that Oscar smiles upon. Traditionally, an actress can win an Academy Award by playing anything from a call girl (Elizabeth Taylor, *Butterfield 8*) to a convicted murderer (Susan Hayward, *I Want to Live*), but motherhood is the one screen image that remains sacred. Just look at the list of past best-actress winners: Joan Crawford (*Mildred Pierce*), Greer Garson (*Mrs. Miniver*), Julie Andrews (*Mary Poppins*), and Katharine Hepburn (*Guess Who's Coming to Dinner?*)—all women whose primary concern was the happiness of the children in their care. The minute Shirley MacLaine climbed into her daughter's crib in the very first scene of *Terms of Endearment*, Oscar was suddenly within her grasp. Poor Mary Tyler Moore. In *Ordinary People* she was a woman who walked away from her family and wasn't even punished for it. How could she possibly compete with Sissy Spacek who, as Loretta Lynn, raised six children while she kept cutting gold records?

In the end, Sissy Spacek—not Mary—won the Oscar, but Mary's moment of triumph came earlier that evening when she appeared onstage at the Dorothy Chandler Pavilion to present the best supporting actor award. Tumultuous applause greeted her as she walked toward the podium, joined by her co-presenter Jack Lemmon. This was Mary's first television appearance since the death of her son, and the irony of the moment was inescapable. When the winner turned out to be Timothy Hutton, her cinema son, and he bounded onstage to receive an Oscar and a hug from Mary, half the audience held their breath and choked back tears.

Later, in the press room, gossip columnist Rona Barrett asked Jack Lemmon if he had any professional advice for Timothy Hutton. Jack seemed irritated by the question and refused to oblige Rona with even a few harmless quotes for her NBC news spot. Mary rushed in to bridge the gap. She took Jack's arm and led him back to Rona, telling him, "Come on, say a few things—make Rona happy."

Mary had always known the value of publicity . . . but in the last few months she had learned the value of kindness, too.

➣ 11 ➢

A New Life

After finishing her run in *Whose Life Is It, Anyway?*, Mary was content to bask in the glow of that success and of her simultaneous triumph in *Ordinary People*. Mary had been through such a devastating cycle of loss—the death of her sister, the breakup of her marriage, the death of her son —that she needed a resting period to find what novelist Willa Cather had once called "the quiet center of my life."

Mary undertook no projects for almost a year. She continued to settle into her new lifestyle in New York, see her analyst regularly, keep up with a few selected friends, and there was a man or two in her life. Right after her separation from Grant Tinker, Mary had been involved briefly with Michael Lindsay-Hogg, her director in *Whose Life*, but that relationship was strictly casual. Then in January 1981 —shortly before she went to Los Angeles for the Academy Award presentations—Mary had met multimillionaire Gordon White at a New York dinner party. At fifty-seven, the well-known British businessman was fourteen years older than Mary and something of an international playboy. Over the years, his past conquests had included Marilyn Monroe, Rita Hayworth, Grace Kelly (prior to her marriage to the Prince of Monaco), Jane Russell, and Susan Hayward. Gordy, as Mary called him, had a penchant for jet-set living, with elegant homes in Britain, New York, and Venezuela, and a stable of about twenty racehorses.

Mary's relationship with Gordon White lasted all the way through the summer and fall of 1981. She flew to England to attend the royal races at Ascot with him, then they went to Paris for another day at the races. In New York they attended Broadway premieres, dined at exclusive restaurants, and became regulars at Xenon's, one of New York's trendier discos. John Bardazzi, manager of Xenon's, told the *Star:* "They've been here a lot over the last year. And, just recently, they showed up three times in the same week." He added that Mary just "loves to dance" and that Sir Gordon had no trouble keeping up with her.

By December of 1981, Mary was back at work—filming *Six Weeks* with Dudley Moore—and her romance with Sir Gordon White was on the wane. For the first time in print, Mary was willing to talk about her son. She told Wayne Warga of the *Los Angeles Times* that what helped her deal with the grief was sitting down and writing a thank-you note to every single person who had sent a message of sympathy. "When I was done," she said, "I was sorry there were no more to answer." She also confided that "I miss him when good things begin to happen . . . he was beginning to be a friend. I was alone, for the first time, and he was very protective of me."

It seemed more than coincidental, then—almost therapeutic perhaps—that Mary chose *Six Weeks* as her first project after Richie's death. In the script written by David Seltzer, Mary played a supersuccessful businesswoman whose young daughter (played by Katherine Healy) is dying of leukemia. Dudley Moore is a congressman who befriends them both during the last months of the daughter's life. Mary maintained, though, that she didn't specifically seek out a screenplay dealing with the death of a child

—she just couldn't turn down *Six Weeks* because the subject was so dramatic and her own role so compelling.

At the same time, Mary hired Lynda Rosen Obst as her own personal film scout. Lynda, who had formerly been a vice president at Polygram Pictures, came to work for MTM Enterprises for the specific purpose of finding novels and story ideas that might lend themselves to being screen vehicles for Mary. The plan was to develop six major motion pictures with Mary in the starring role. Mary still had a commitment to CBS to return to that network in the fall of 1981, possibly in a new situation-comedy series, but Mary managed to get that commitment put on hold. In fact, she had already decided in her own mind never to return to TV on a weekly basis. A series of any kind was definitely out. "No more television unless some very special movie of the week comes along," she told Wayne Warga. To Mary's way of thinking, most made-for-TV movies didn't have the scope or emotional depth to make it as feature films and that's why they wound up on television. Within two years, though, she'd change her mind about that.

Making *Six Weeks* was a low-keyed experience, compared to what had been demanded of her in *Ordinary People* or *Whose Life*. Despite the morbid nature of the subject, the story was told with great restraint and little pathos. Mary had a pleasant relationship with both her co-star, Dudley Moore, and her director, Tony Bill, but it was child actress Katherine Healy who really stole her heart. Katherine was a talented ballerina, and she and Mary would often work out together. Mary admitted to "twinges of jealousy," because, looking at Katherine, she saw herself again as a child and remembered all her own ambitions as a dancer.

While *Six Weeks* filmed in Los Angeles, Mary lived in the Bel Air house that she and Grant had shared only briefly.

But she planned to return to New York permanently once filming was completed, so she was thrilled when Grant offered to buy the house from her. Since the divorce, they had remained friendly; and now that Grant had left MTM to become head of NBC, Hollywood observers began to wonder if he might indeed be able to lure Mary back to television in a new series—on a new network.

By mid-1982 there was a new man in Mary's life, a forty-two-year-old New York public relations expert named Ed Menken. They had been introduced by a mutual friend, and the relationship deepened when Ed was able to do a personal favor for Mary. That September her parents were planning to visit Rome, and Mary was hoping to arrange a papal audience for them. A personal friend of Ed's, Monsignor O'Brien, was able to facilitate the audience; and Ed and Mary wound up in Rome together, sightseeing with Mary's parents.

According to the tabloids, who rushed to follow Mary everywhere, "Mary behaved like an infatuated teenager. She was forever giving him little kisses on the cheek, and reaching for his hand." That same paper reported that Ed Menken acted "more like a son-in-law than a boyfriend" around Mary's parents and that Ed and Mary behaved "almost as if they were on their honeymoon."

After Ed Menken faded into the background, Mary was linked with comedian Steve Martin, who escorted Mary to the star-studded premiere of *Six Weeks* in December 1982. The romance, along with the film, wasn't destined for a long run. Apparently Steve and Mary had been introduced by a mutual friend (the agent who represents them both) and their dates were mainly a series of publicity occasions. The fact that the relationship was strictly casual didn't stop the press from predicting an engagement and making headlines out of the fact that, at thirty-seven, Steve was eight years younger than Mary.

Dating a "wild and crazy guy" like Steve Martin was probably the best medicine for Mary at the moment. The public and critical reception of *Six Weeks* was hardly enthusiastic, and the film didn't fare well at the box-office, despite the fact that Dudley Moore's past movies, *10* and *Arthur*, had both turned out to be blockbusters. Undoubtedly, the subject matter of the film had a great deal to do with its failure. *Six Weeks* seemed to deal with every human emotion except the one we all cling to the most—hope. The last scene was particularly depressing—Katherine Healy succumbs to a fatal attack during a subway ride in Manhattan and dies while Mary futilely bangs on the doors and windows of the car, trying to get the train to stop. There is no postscript. Mary and Dudley Moore don't get together in the wake of this tragedy; the child's death has accomplished nothing. No wonder moviegoers didn't stampede the theater lines to see this film during the Christmas season of 1982. It was hardly brimming with Christmas cheer.

Perhaps, too, moviegoers had already had their fill of child-related tragedies. Earlier in 1982, Jack Lemmon had futilely searched for his murdered son in *Missing*, and the horror of Meryl Streep's separation from her children in a Nazi death camp was a climactic part of *Sophie's Choice*. By the time Christmas came, people were much more eager to watch Dustin Hoffman's funny antics in *Tootsie* and the wonder of the supernatural in *E.T.*

The poor reception of *Six Weeks* seemed to put Mary's movie career on hold once again, but this time Mary was more philosophical about it. As she celebrated her forty-fifth birthday, she recognized the fact that she was probably not going to win a second Oscar nomination for this film, and that at this point in her life other movie roles might not be that easy to negotiate.

Movies were changing—and while the late 1970s and early '80s had been something of a golden time for women in films, drama was now at a low ebb on the silver screen. With cable TV and the video-cassette revolution, adults were content to stay home and watch movies. Only kids and teenagers were filling up the movie theaters, and the new money-makers were space epics like *Return of the Jedi* and teen trash films like *Fast Times at Ridgemont High* and *Porky's*. Even a two-time Academy Award winner like Jane Fonda was turning to a made-for-television project (*The Dollmaker* for ABC), and Robert Redford hadn't made a film since *Ordinary People*.

It's interesting to note that Redford, Fonda, and Mary Tyler Moore—whose careers have all taken similar leaps and dips—were all born in the same year, 1937. In fact, Jane, who was born on December 21, 1937, is only eight days older than Mary. Whether by accident or astrological design, their careers have run strangely parallel. Jane was destined to grow up and become one of the most influential women in motion pictures, just as Mary would someday dominate television. Redford helped make a star out of Jane Fonda when they teamed up in the 1967 feature *Barefoot in the Park*, and he turned Mary into a cinema actress in *Ordinary People*.

But Jane Fonda and Mary Tyler Moore had a lot more in common than their mutual admiration for Robert Redford. They both started out in show business as light and frothy all-American types—two kids who looked perfect for a Pepsodent ad—and wound up changing their images radically over the years. In 1961, when newcomer Mary was playing a helpless suburban wife on *The Dick Van Dyke Show*, Jane was cast in a similar mold in the movie *Period of Adjustment* after proving that she could be a thoroughly disarming cheerleader in the Tony Perkins comedy *Tall Story*. Staying cute (and nonthreatening) paid off for both ladies all through the 1960s. It brought Mary two Emmies for *Van Dyke* and it launched Jane as a comic sex kitten in films like *Cat Ballou* and *Any Wednesday*. In 1967, for example, when Mary was a paragon of perkiness in *Thoroughly Modern Millie*, Jane matched her smile for smile in *Barefoot in the Park*, and both films ranked among the year's biggest box-office hits.

By the end of the 1960s, though, no two women could have been further apart. Mary—up to her ears in needlepoint—was happily married to Grant Tinker and just about as Republican as they come; Jane—after dissolving her marriage to French director Roger Vadim—had drifted into the politics of protest and was under surveillance by the FBI for her involvement with the radical left. Yet, for all their differences in style and ideology, Mary Tyler Moore and Jane Fonda had more in common than either of them realized. For they were the trendsetters, the two women who would shake up show business the most.

As the 1970s dawned, Jane Fonda emerged as the key movie actress of the new decade—and Mary Tyler Moore carved out the same territory for herself in television. Both were turning away from the kind of frivolous performances that had been their stock in trade. Both were in the process of evolving into serious actresses and bringing a new sense of purpose and commitment to their work. Jane proved herself a dramatic virtuoso in films like *They Shoot Horses, Don't They?* and *Klute*. At the same time, Mary was bringing TV comedy out of the dark ages and creating a weekly series that could be sensitive, adult, and funny, too.

All through the 1970s, Mary Tyler Moore was *the* preeminent television personality, just as Jane Fonda was *the* dominant film star. And once again both women were wise enough to know when to move on. In the 1980s, Jane began edging away from film acting and branching out as a businesswoman: promoting her exercise book and workout program, co-producing and packaging her own TV show, *9 to 5*. Meanwhile, Mary was hungry for new challenges, too. Rather than simply recycle herself in a third situation-comedy series, she went after more demanding roles in far tougher arenas. The results were *Whose Life Is It, Anyway?* and *Ordinary People*.

Ironically, even their mutual obsession with exercise has a certain strain of similarity. Mary became an exercise fanatic as part of her diabetes treatment program; for Jane it was a way to overcome bulimia. And even when it comes to politics, they're no longer poles apart. As Jane Fonda's political views have becoming increasingly moderate, Mary has deserted the Republican party in favor of the Democrats and become an avid supporter of the Equal Rights Amendment.

Many things about Mary's lifestyle have been surprising and seemingly out of character in recent years. Since leaving Grant Tinker, she's become far less inhibited, more willing to take risks professionally and personally. Mary, who once hated New York and felt frightened and vulnerable there during her *Breakfast at Tiffany's* stint, has done a complete turnabout. She now bicycles regularly in Central Park and remembers Los Angeles with barely a flicker of regret. And the same lady who approached psychoanalysis with silent resistance in the 1960s is now intensely devoted to her New York analyst (whom she visits weekly in the Gramercy Park section of Manhattan). Asked if she'll ever finish therapy, Mary sighs and says, "No, I don't think I'll ever give that up. For me, it's a need like doing the cross-word puzzle in the Sunday *New York Times*."

But none of the transformations in her life have been as baffling as her decision, in the fall of 1983, to marry for the third time. Anybody attempting to become Mary Tyler Moore's husband would have met with public disapproval, perhaps—half the country thought she was still married to Grant Tinker, the other half considered her Mrs. Dick Van Dyke—but Mary's announcement that she had fallen in love with Dr. Robert Levine, a Jewish cardiologist fifteen years her junior, stunned everyone. The celebrity press bit into the story with relish and wrote about Mary's May-December romance with the same kind of oh-she-can't-be-serious-can-she? attitude that it usually saves for Bianca Jagger and Elizabeth Taylor. Mary had suddenly slipped out of sainthood. The tabloids, reveling in the younger man–older woman aspect of the romance, enjoyed pointing out that Mary and her boyish bridegroom seemed about as compatible as bagels and lox smeared with Miracle Whip.

Through it all, Mary never lost her smile. In public, she remained as upbeat as ever. Did she mind being plastered all over the front page of the supermarket tabloids? No, not at all. Even this kind of publicity had some redeeming value, if it broke down a few barriers, if it made people feel a little more comfortable about relationships that defy the norm. But Mary knew that she and Robert were hardly "ordinary people," and in private she anguished over the headlines that painted her as a desperate case. No, she was not a lost lady clutching at one last chance for happiness after every other relationship in her life had gone sour.

Poor Mary. If Elizabeth Taylor had announced that she was moving in with Boy George, the press probably would have been more sympathetic. After all, we expect Liz to do wild, impulsive things like that, but not Mary Tyler Moore. Mary, to most of us, was still the perfect all-American girl. We think of her forever serene and cool, with her back, like the crease in her tennis whites and the stitches of her needlepoint, perfectly straight.

From the outside looking in, there was definitely something out-of-kilter about the Mary-Robert scenario. This was a match pulled out of a Joan Rivers routine, but certainly not made in heaven. Let's face it, who could ever have imagined *goyishe* Mary—no matter how good a sport she was—standing under a *chupah* (Jewish wedding canopy) while the groom nervously smashed a wine glass with his foot and the guests shouted, *"Mazel tov!"* Rhoda Morgenstern should have been the bride, not Mary. If Mary had to marry again at all, we pictured some distinguished, middle-aged WASP—who looked like Richard Crenna in *First, You Cry* or James Garner in *Heartsounds*—not a thirty-year-old medical resident from Mount Sinai Hospital.

People magazine alleged that Mary's "close chums" were in shock. In an article in the December 5, 1983, issue of *People*, one unidentified source called Levine "a big bore" and "unattractive." Another cattily remarked: "I saw her entwined with that shlub on Columbus Avenue. What does she see in him?" The *Star* described Levine as "tall, dark and handsome," but added that he had been fifty to sixty pounds overweight when he first met Mary.

Maybe Robert Levine didn't radiate movie-star macho, but in Mary's eyes, at least, he definitely had other qualities that were far more precious. From the start, Mary was struck by his intelligence and sensitivity, and she was especially charmed by his medical manner. Ever since she'd become diabetic, Mary had been making the rounds from one doctor to another, and what she had often encountered was smugness and arrogance. Robert Levine was different. He was quiet, but warm and courteous. Rarely, in all her years spent in doctors' offices, had Mary encountered a physician who treated his patients in such a forceful, yet caring way, as Robert did.

It was illness—not Mary's but her mother's—that first brought them together. In October 1982, Mary's mother, Marjorie Moore, had just returned from Europe and was staying with Mary in New York. During the trip, she had come down with a bad bronchial infection, but didn't want to make a fuss about it. By the time Mary saw her, she was running a high fever (and Mary suspected that her hypertension was flaring up as well).

At first, her mom refused to see a doctor, but Mary was insistent. The trouble was that Mary's own physician happened to be Jewish, and Mrs. Moore had taken ill right in the middle of the Jewish High Holy Day period. When Mary called her doctor, he was at Yom Kippur services, and she was referred by his answering service to Levine, who was standing in for him. Even though Levine was Jewish, too, he obviously wasn't very religious if he was willing to work on a holiday like Yom Kippur—the Day of Atonement and the holiest day of the year in the Jewish calendar.

Being a very lapsed Catholic herself, Mary was intrigued by Levine's less-than-intense approach to religious observances. Later, when they spoke on the phone for the first time, she was even more impressed at the way Levine handled her mother. When Levine called in response to the message Mary had left with her own doctor's answering service, she told him about her mother's bronchial problems and hypertension. She also mentioned that Marjorie Moore was a feisty patient. Levine said, "Let me speak to her," and in less than a minute somehow had Mrs. Moore practically eating out of his hand. He convinced her to be at Mount Sinai Hospital in half an hour flat for emergency tests.

Obviously, despite his boyish phone manner, Mary's

mother trusted him implicitly. Mary went with her to Mount Sinai, and the man they met proved to be even more charming in person. Levine in the flesh was even younger than Mary had imagined, but that impression didn't last very long. Levine had a take-charge personality, at least where medical matters were concerned. He was unassuming and soft-spoken, but somehow he had nurses and interns scrambling to carry out his orders. He took his time examining Mrs. Moore and made both ladies feel that he had all the time in the world, just for them. After prescribing treatment, he chatted amiably with them for a few minutes and Mary was pleased to discover that, unlike some doctors, Robert Levine took a lively interest in things well beyond the bounds of medicine. He had Mary in stitches (figuratively speaking, that is) as he described the trials and tribulations of making his singing debut at a recent hospital party. Mary, who is certainly no stranger to musical ups and downs herself, told him she understood his stage fright thoroughly. Later, she described him to friends as "an extraordinary, totally delightful man."

Mary and Robert Levine were just in the process of getting to know each other when her movie *Six Weeks* premiered. In that film she played a successful woman (a cosmetics manufacturer) who fell in love with a married congressional candidate (Dudley Moore). It was her daughter's terminal illness that brought them together. Ironically, in real life, it was Mary's mom who wound up playing matchmaker, although, thankfully, her medical problems were very treatable.

Without intending it, Marjorie Moore became the catalyst for bringing Mary and Robert Levine together over a period of several weeks. Chances are—because of their fifteen-year age difference and the fact that they traveled in two totally opposite worlds—left to their own devices, they never would have gone beyond step one. But over the next few weeks, as she regained her strength, Marjorie Moore needed to see Levine on a regular basis, and Mary always accompanied her to Levine's office. In a way, without anyone planning it, her follow-up visits became an excuse for Mary and Robert to keep on seeing each other. Mary could have stayed in the waiting room while her mother was being examined, but, like any concerned daughter, she had medical questions to ask about her mother's condition. For his part, Robert Levine always seemed particularly pleased that Mary had come along.

Pretty soon they were on a first-name basis and making small talk about everything from tennis to theater. Once, Robert remarked that Mary looked pale and fatigued. She explained that she was diabetic and that this was one of her low days. Robert, of course, understood instantly. He told her to feel free—if her own doctor was ever unavailable— to call him, at any hour, day or night, if she ever had a problem with her diet or her medication. His exact words were, "If there's any kind of emergency—even if it's the middle of the night—just call me." Was he referring only to a medical emergency? Mary jokingly asked him if "acute loneliness" qualified as an emergency, too. He replied, smiling but very serious, that he couldn't think of a better reason to be awakened at two A.M.

That conversation was definitely a turning point in their relationship, but neither of them knew quite how to proceed. The attraction on both their parts was obviously very strong, but did either of them feel brave enough to risk a romantic involvement? Mary had no frame of reference about how to behave in a situation like this. Nothing in her own life had prepared her for it. Her two previous husbands, both older than she was, had done all the pursuing when they courted her. And none of the men she had dated since divorcing Grant Tinker were in any way similar to Robert Levine. They were all actors or directors—showbiz types who could charm their way through any relationship, glib and smooth and never at an awkward loss for words.

But Robert Levine was different in every way possible. He was substantially younger than Mary. He was Jewish. He was a brilliant cardiologist, but a total "civilian" when it came to show business. What did they really have in common? After their last conversation, Mary resolved to put him out of her mind. Maybe it really was just a case of "acute loneliness" that had made him seem so attractive. He was, after all, only a few years older than Richie had been.

A few days went by, and Mary felt in more of a dilemma than ever. Whatever the attraction was—and she couldn't really pin a name on it—it refused to subside. The more determined she was to forget Dr. Robert Levine, the more he intruded on her thoughts. "My God, this is impossible," someone else in Mary's situation might have thought. "I'm like a schoolgirl with a stupid crush." Someone else might have written him off as a ridiculous longshot. Mary couldn't do that, but that's as far as it went. She didn't phone Robert and he didn't phone her. Maybe he wasn't ready to push things either. Maybe he had simply lost interest in her. Yet Mary remembered very clearly his invitation to call at any time. That wasn't just a polite brush-off. He had certainly sounded sincere. At the time, he had probably meant it. Mary felt pretty sure about that. Maybe he was just battling the same doubts she was.

Mary knew there were only two alternatives: she could take the initiative and phone Robert, or she could let the whole thing drop. Chances are, if she didn't make the first move, that would be the end of it. Mary sensed that Robert had already gone as far as he felt comfortable going. The next move was up to her. What did she have to lose?

Finding the courage to call him was probably one of the hardest things Mary ever had to do. Unless she feigned illness—and that seemed like a particularly ridiculous maneuver—there was no way she could call without laying her personal feelings on the line. She might get hurt, or at the very least embarrassed. He might even be involved with someone else, for all she knew. Mary played out the various scenarios in her mind over and over again—she even hashed it out with her therapist—and finally she decided not to let Robert's invitation pass.

If Mary Richards had made the call, she probably would have been blushing from head to toe. That's exactly how Mary felt as she dialed Robert Levine's number. Actually, at that moment, for the first time in her life, she was probably wishing she could turn into Rhoda Morgenstern, not Mary Richards. How to get a Jewish doctor to go out with you? It was one situation that Rhoda could probably handle a lot better than Mary.

There was only one way Mary could tackle this phone call: she tried to be as straightforward as possible. She asked him if he knew how to cook. When he said no, she suggested—trying to keep it as light as possible—that he'd simply have to take her out to dinner.

The very next night Robert rang Mary's doorbell and escorted her out to dinner. Whether they dined on Chinese food or not remains their little secret, but whatever the cuisine, long before the last course, they both knew what their fortune was.

❧ 12 ❧

Whose Wedding Is It, Anyway?

No matter how you slice it, fifteen years is a substantial age difference between a woman and a man.

Mary was in high school when Robert Levine was born; he was still a toddler when she was already married for the first time and raising a child of her own; and he hadn't even been bar-mitzvahed when she was winning Emmies for her comedy antics on *The Dick Van Dyke Show*.

Mary would be the first to admit that, as close as they are in some ways, the crucial ways, in other matters they will always be a generation apart. Mary was raised on Ginger Rogers and Fred Astaire movies; Robert grew up with Bob Dylan and the Beatles. Occasionally, Mary will mention the name of a 1940s movie star—Sonja Henie or Virginia Mayo—and Robert will stare at her blankly. Show business isn't his sphere to begin with, and these are people who had their biggest rush of success a decade before he was born.

History tells us that, in spite of the obstacles, older women and younger men often make excellent bedfellows. British Prime Minister Disraeli enjoyed a long and enduring marriage to a woman many years his senior. Ruth Gordon and Garson Kanin—another May-December match—remained married over thirty years. Today it's still uncommon, but hardly unheard-of, for women in their late thirties to be romantically involved with men in their early twenties. Olivia Newton-John was thirty-six when she finally wed her twenty-five-year-old lover, Matt Lattanzi.

Much of the prejudice, of course, stems from a double standard. Middle-aged men have always been free to marry younger women and society barely raises an eyebrow. The fact that women in Mary Tyler Moore's age group are now turning the tables and robbing the cradle, so to speak, may just be another sign of women catching up with men and demanding equal rights. In Mary's case, her involvement with Robert Levine seems particularly pointed. At the same time that Robert and Mary were falling in love, her fifty-seven-year-old ex-husband, Grant Tinker, was engaged in a highly publicized romance with Melanie Burke, a girlish-looking brunette who was young enough to be Mary's daughter.

Nevertheless, the public still has mixed feelings about young men romancing older women. *Dynasty*'s Joan Collins—perhaps television's only fifty-one-year-old sex kitten —is often successfully paired with younger leading men, and her TV movie, *Making of a Male Model*, with the late Jon-Erik Hexum, was a huge hit. But *Dallas* ran into trouble when it tried to team svelte and fortyish Linda Gray with teen idol Christopher Atkins, and the romance was dropped after a season.

Of all the top women in television, Mary Tyler Moore is perhaps hardest to picture in a relationship with a younger man. In her career, she's always leaned toward mature-looking men, usually several years her senior. All three male regulars on *The Mary Tyler Moore*—Ed Asner, Ted Knight, and Gavin MacLeod—were hardly boyish in looks or personality; and Donald Sutherland (*Ordinary People*), James Garner (*Heartsounds*), and Robert Preston (*Finnegan, Begin Again*) were equally middle-aged.

Who could picture Mary teaming with Mel Gibson or

Richard Gere? It almost defies credibility, perhaps because Mary—more than almost any other actress—has always seemed so level-headed, down-to-earth, and all-American. Her real-life encounter with Dr. Robert Levine was the first time Mary's off-screen behavior ever openly clashed with the public's perception of her. All that had happened in her life previously was either tragic or triumphant, but never so candidly unconventional.

After becoming acquainted in the fall of 1982, Mary and Robert spent New Year's Eve together and dated all through the spring of 1983. From the start, the attraction was stronger than either of them was willing to admit, and time only intensified it. They found it easy to talk to each other, to communicate, and to share things. Mary enjoyed Robert's warm sense of humor, and it was refreshing to be with him after so many years of being friends, exclusively, with people in show business.

By the summer, they were sharing a weekend beach house in Quogue, one of Long Island's most fashionable resorts. Mary was between professional commitments (in fact, she was debating what her next career move should be) and she was able to lavish all her time and energy on the relationship. It was obvious that she and Robert were serious about each other and, although they knew neither of their families would be thrilled by the prospect, they began looking ahead toward building a permanent life together. In September, back in Manhattan, Mary began to investigate Robert's faith. On Rosh Hashanah (the Jewish New Year), she attended Reform services with him at Temple Emanu-El on Fifth Avenue; at the same time, Mary began taking instruction in Reform Judaism. She had no plans to convert, but felt it might smooth things over with Robert's family, who obviously had mixed feelings about the match.

Although Mary's parents were both devout Catholics,

there was no possibility that Robert would convert. More-over, with two divorces behind her, Mary couldn't be mar-ried in church under any circumstances. Her parents seemed to accept all that, and were genuinely concerned about only one thing—Mary's happiness. If Robert loved her, that was all that mattered. Of course, it also helped that Robert was Marjorie Moore's doctor. He had won her trust long before he and Mary had even thought of dating.

Robert's family took a little more convincing. To have expected anything else would have been unrealistic. After all, Mary—twice divorced, non-Jewish, diabetic, and well past her child-bearing years—was hardly the kind of future daughter-in-law they'd envisioned him bringing home.

There were arguments which Mary found unsettling at first, but enlightening in the long run. It was her first experience with a Jewish family, and there was no escaping the fact that the family's attitudes and traditions were far different from anything she could remember in her own background. Watching Robert and his relatives "discuss" things, Mary learned that in a Jewish family it's all right to raise your voice, yell a little, let off steam, and apologize later. Nobody gets offended, at least not permanently. In her family, where politeness and so-called "civilized behav-ior" were valued above all else, such scenes never would have been permissible. In her parents' house, people dis-cussed things calmly and rationally, and when it was no longer possible to keep cool, they stormed out, slammed the door, and retreated from the situation. In the Levine house, nobody left the room till the argument was settled. That kind of emotional free-for-all was hard to take at first—and Mary didn't know whether to stand up and leave or join in, too. But once she got the hang of these kinds of family discussions, Mary found it a healthy change—and even began to draw close to her future in-laws. It was much better, Mary realized, to release her feelings than to keep them bottled up inside. That was a mistake she'd made too often in her other marriages.

This time, Mary vowed, silence would never be a weapon in her relationship with Robert. They would talk things out and share a real marriage of equals. That was what had been lacking in her other marriages. Twice before Mary had chosen as husbands older men who tended to dominate rather than complement her. This time she wasn't looking for a substitute father, or an off-screen director, or a gladiator to do battle for her. She wanted an equal partner, and Robert shared her feelings completely on that point. He wasn't interested in a woman who would stand in his shadow or bend completely to his will. In that sense, his age was a definite plus. Because he was only thirty and part of a generation that takes women's independence for granted, Robert's concept of marriage was less confining than if he'd been one of Mary's contemporaries. Mary's success neither threatened nor intimidated him. Marrying a woman with a career was something he'd always planned to do.

By November, Robert's family had given their blessings and all of Mary's close friends knew that a wedding was in the offing. Dasha Epstein, one of the producers of *Whose Life Is It, Anyway?*, gave Mary a Park Avenue bridal shower, inviting her eight closest friends, among them actresses Pippa Scott and Hope Lange. They all brought Mary gag gifts like alarm clocks (to wake Robert up in the middle of the night for emergency calls) and stethoscopes.

The wedding took place on November 23, 1983. It was a Reform Jewish ceremony with a reception for friends and relatives afterward. Mingling with Robert's family and his medical associates was a liberal sprinkling of West Coast television stars. One guest quipped that Mary's wedding looked "like a cross between an AMA convention and *Night of a Hundred Stars.*" The Hollywood contingent included Linda Gray, Hope Lange, Brenda Vaccaro, Martin Mull, Dick Cavett, Barbara Walters, and several of Mary's former *MTM* castmates—Ted Knight, Valerie Harper, Georgia Engel, and Cloris Leachman. Despite his friendly divorce from Mary, Grant Tinker did not attend the wedding, but he did wire the couple his best wishes.

Mary looked radiant in a peach-colored antique lace dress with a high collar and puffed sleeves. Robert was equally handsome in a stylishly cut dark, pinstriped suit. Beverly Sanders (who had played Valerie Harper's constantly pregnant friend on *Rhoda*) was Mary's matron of honor, and Robert's brother, Michael Levine, was best man. Mary's father gave her away.

Rabbi Richard Chapin, who was Mary's religious instructor at Temple Emanu-El, performed the ceremony and helped the couple recite their vows in Hebrew. At one point in the ceremony both Mary's parents and Robert's bowed their heads as the rabbi asked all the guests to pray for a happy life together for these newlyweds.

After Mary and Robert exchanged rings under the *chupah*, the rabbi wrapped a wine glass in a linen handkerchief and placed it on the floor for the groom to break. After Robert smashed it with his foot, the guests all shouted, *"Mazel tov!"* ("Good luck!") and Robert kissed his bride. Mary's first words after the ceremony were, "This is the happiest day of my life!"

More than anything, Mary's wedding seemed to imply that her move to New York was final and permanent. With Robert on staff at Mount Sinai Hospital and Mary firm in her desire not to allow too many work separations to intrude on this marriage, returning to the West Coast was definitely out of the question. Earlier that year, Mary had told friends that she was indeed anxious to do comedy again, and Grant Tinker—in his bid to bolster NBC's programming line-up—was reportedly hoping to lure Mary back to the tube in her own weekly situation-comedy series again. But now there was no way that Mary could accept that offer. Doing a TV series in Los Angeles would mean a commuting marriage, a prospect that she dreaded.

On her wedding day, one tabloid reported that Mary intended to tone down her career considerably now that she was Mrs. Robert Levine. She reportedly said, "I want to play the role of perfect housewife to my doctor husband. It's the most important role I've ever played." It hardly seemed likely that Mary, who frankly detested home-making, would suddenly turn into a contented domestic drudge, but perhaps there was a tongue-in-cheek element in what she told the press that day. And who could blame her if she was having a little fun with reporters? After all, it had been such a long time since Mary had had reason to joke with the press.

Unlike Mary's 1962 wedding to Grant Tinker in Las Vegas, which was virtually ignored by the press, Mary's third marriage was a media event of some note. Although no TV cameras were permitted to view the ceremony, reporters gathered outside and managed to corner several of the guests both arriving and departing. Robert's family was hardly camera-shy. "We're so happy to have Mary in our family," one of Robert's relatives bubbled to an NBC news team. "She's a wonderful, wonderful girl," another relative echoed, smiling directly into the camera.

All three major networks covered the wedding in their nightly news reports. Somebody quipped that the only thing missing was Ted Baxter mispronouncing everybody's name or maybe Sue Ann Nivens trying to kidnap the best man. Ah, but what did those critics know? Mary, beaming with happiness that night, was suddenly our old Mary, full of hope and optimism again. She was calmer and less anxious than she had been in years; she had truly put the dark times behind her now, and Robert, attentive to her every move and glance, was obviously deeply in love. They weren't the typical bride and groom on the wedding cake, but their devotion was surprisingly real. Besides, in the last analysis, whose wedding was it, anyway?

❧ 13 ❧

Doctor's Wife

Mary Tyler Moore was no stranger to marriage—indeed, she had been somebody's wife nearly all her adult life—but marriage to young Dr. Robert Levine was an entirely different matter.

For one thing, they were rarely apart. During their first few months together, Mary stayed close to home—and was apparently happy to do so. She had a far different attitude toward not working than she had had when she became Mrs. Grant Tinker. "I don't feel so driven anymore," Mary said. "I can go for twenty minutes now without searching for something to do."

In 1963, when Mary was first married to Grant, they only saw each other on occasional weekends. He had taken over as vice president in charge of programming for NBC; she was working on *The Dick Van Dyke Show* in Los Angeles. "I get to see more of Dick Van Dyke than I see my own husband," Mary had sighed, trying to make light of a difficult situation. When Grant and Mary were first dating, they had spent a whirlwind week in New York together—Mary was in town promoting *The Dick Van Dyke Show*—and they'd had dinner and seen a play or gone dancing every night of the week. "Then I had to go back to California," Mary told a reporter for the *New York Post*. "It was the first of our separations and we've had many since then. It's dreadful and it gets worse and worse and worse." Mary admitted that she and Grant phoned each other long-distance so often that their monthly phone bill was $500. "I'd be better off owning stock in AT&T," she joked.

Mary was determined not to repeat this pattern when she married Robert Levine, so she shied away from accepting job offers that would take her too far away from home for too long. The major priority in her life now was her marriage, not her career, and for Mary, who'd been pointing herself in the direction of stardom since early childhood, this represented a radical change of heart indeed.

After becoming Mrs. Robert Levine, Mary continued to make headlines, but only with Robert at her side. On December 18, 1983, less than a month after the nuptials, the *New York Daily News* reported that "the two have been all over town . . . billing and cooing and doing all those things people in love just love to do." One night, for instance, the newlyweds went to see the Broadway play *Noises Off,* then had a late supper at Sardi's where the paparazzi who hang around Broadway caught up with them. Mary, as usual, was puffing away on a cigarette, but Robert admonished photographers not to snap her till she put the cigarette out. "We all know smoking is bad for your health," he told them. "Mary wouldn't want to be seen in print that way. It might look like she was encouraging other people to take up the habit."

Although Mary couldn't quit smoking and was still drinking more than she should, Robert's influence on her was definitely making her more health-conscious. In 1984 she became national spokesman for the Juvenile Diabetes Foundation and worked closely with *Days of Our Lives* star Gloria Loring (whose son is diabetic) as a celebrity fundraiser. Mary ran into an unexpected problem, though. In the past, Mary had been an active supporter in the battle to prevent cruelty to animals. Now, some of these pro-animal groups were petitioning the California legislature to outlaw the use of animals for experimental purposes in diabetes research. According to prevailing medical opinion, the use of animals is crucial in insulin research; and although Mary is an animal lover, she felt that finding a cure for diabetes has to be a priority. As Gloria Loring told her, "I have to believe what the doctors tell me. Without them, my son wouldn't be here today."

In the spring of 1984, Mary agreed to star in the ABC-TV movie *Heartsounds*, which would necessitate her first separation from Robert. *Heartsounds* (based on the bestseller by Martha Weinman Lear) was due to be shot partially in Manhattan (where the story actually takes place) and partially in Toronto, Canada (where an apartment house was being temporarily converted to resemble the West Side Manhattan building where Martha and her husband actually lived).

Mary was immediately intrigued by the project. The book was a documentary account of Hal Lear's prolonged battle with heart disease, his disillusionment with the medical profession (Lear was a doctor himself), and his eventual death. Since the story is told through his wife Martha's eyes, much of *Heartsounds* focuses on the Lears' marriage and how it changes during the course of Hal's deterioration.

The TV movie was being produced by Norman Lear (who had been Hal's first cousin), and ABC was hoping to air the project during the fall of 1984. The director was Glenn Jordan, whose last project was the Marsha Mason movie *Only When I Laugh*, a comedy-drama about alcoholism and a mother's alienation from her teenage daughter. In that film, Jordan had effectively lightened the somber mood of the script by casting comic actors—James Coco and Joan Hackett—in key roles. He hoped to do the same with *Heartsounds*, realizing that an unrelieved two-hour TV presentation on heart disease might be more than the average viewer could take. So it was Jordan's idea to add a little warmth and lightness to the piece by casting James Garner and Mary Tyler Moore as Hal and Martha Lear.

Curiously enough, except for a brief chat at a party twenty years before, Mary Tyler Moore and James Garner had never really met. True, they had a few mutual friends and professional acquaintances—Julie Andrews among them. Garner came to *Heartsounds* right after co-starring with Julie in *Victor/Victoria*. Mary had kept up a semi-friendship with Julie Andrews ever since they'd worked together in *Thoroughly Modern Millie*. Before the first rehearsal, Mary didn't know what to expect. Garner had a reputation for being gruff. He was, after all, in the midst of suing Universal Pictures for $22.5 million, which he claimed they owed him in residuals for his hit TV series *The Rockford Files*.

Despite their mutual background in television, both stars came to the production with very different outlooks. Mary, who still treasured her privacy on the set, would retreat to her dressing room as soon as each scene was done. Garner, on the other hand, would hang around the set, joking and making small talk with the crew. He was one of the guys; Mary kept herself aloof and apart. But they managed to strike just the right chords with each other as far as making the movie was concerned. They quickly became, in a sense, Hal and Martha Lear, a long-married couple, needling each other a little from time to time, but affectionate and fiercely devoted to each other nonetheless. Mary, for instance, was always kidding Jim about his supposed "diet"—she constantly caught him sneak-eating during rehearsal breaks.

Garner, in turn, would make a mock grimace and tell the crew, "That lady is such a nag. She never leaves me alone."

In some ways, *Heartsounds* was far easier than a show like *Rockford Files,* where the fights and stunt work took a constant physical toll on the actors. But emotionally it was a draining experience. The script contained 267 scenes, chronicling the Lears' life from Hal's first heart attack to his death. It was chilling subject matter, and by the time the crew was ready to wrap things up in Toronto, Mary couldn't wait to get back to Manhattan and Garner was equally anxious to head home to LA.

There were other distractions, which only intensified the somber mood of the script. During filming, Garner got word that his father had suffered a minor stroke. In addition to that, one night an electrical fire broke out at the hotel where the whole cast was staying. Mary's suite was on the fifteenth floor, and Jim's was one flight above. Fortunately, on his way down to the street, he decided to stop off at Mary's suite. She hadn't heard the alarm. One of her neighbors was banging on her door, but Mary was still sleeping. When Garner arrived and started pounding on the door, too, Mary finally woke up. With Garner's help, she walked down fifteen flights of stairs in her nightgown and made it to the street just in time. Passersby who glimpsed her shivering in the street that night couldn't understand why she was wearing a robe, nightgown, and high heels. They didn't know that Mary, the perennially perfect organizer, had forgotten to pack a pair of bedroom slippers when she came to Toronto. "I had nothing else to wear but my high heels," she says.

As far as the character of Martha Weinman Lear went, Mary seemed tailor-made for the role. Martha, a successful New York writer, was in some ways reminiscent of Betty Rollin, the TV journalist Mary had portrayed so skillfully in *First, You Cry*. Moreover, Martha Lear was a doctor's wife, just as Mary now was; and the fact that Robert Levine's specialty was cardiac rehabilitation made him an invaluable source of knowledge and advice in helping Mary create the role. (Although Robert couldn't leave Mount Sinai Hospital for an extended period of time, he did fly up to Toronto to spend a weekend with Mary, and was on the set a good deal of the time.)

In one crucial way, however, Mary Tyler Moore was nothing like Martha Lear. Mary is a perfectionist about housekeeping—Martha is not. At first Mary found it difficult to play scenes in the Lear apartment with newspapers thrown around the room and pillows tossed on the floor. Mary's instinct was to straighten things up, but when Martha Weinman Lear actually visited the set, she thought it looked too neat. Mary had to learn to relax and enjoy the clutter.

Interestingly enough, although Mary has learned to cope with her own disease (diabetes), she felt she could never be as brave as Martha was in dealing with Hal's illness. Mary wasn't sure she could be that strong in real life, and perhaps that's why the role was so challenging for her. The hardest scenes came after Hal survived open-heart surgery, but suffered brain damage as a result. Mary doubted that in a such a situation she could have been as strong as Martha was. "I probably would have caved in," she says.

Both Mary and James Garner gave far more sensitive performances than they ever had in television before, and *Heartsounds* was a critical success when it aired on ABC. Later, *TV Guide*'s Judith Crist—the dean of video critics—picked *Heartsounds* as one of the ten best television films of 1984. According to Crist, it went "far beyond the clichés of life-and-death medical dramas to offer us a mature couple, portrayed by Mary Tyler Moore and James Garner, exercising their particular brand of valor in facing the recurrent crises of coping with a fatal illness."

As the 1984–85 TV season came to a close, both Mary and Garner seemed likely to win Emmy nominations for their work in *Heartsounds*. Mary's strongest competition would probably be Farrah Fawcett for *The Burning Bed*, Ann-Margret for *A Streetcar Named Desire*, and Jane Seymour for *The Sun Also Rises*. Garner would undoubtedly be racing against veteran George C. Scott (*A Christmas Carol*) and newcomer Gary Cole (*Fatal Vision*).

Except for the near brush with fire, Mary had truly enjoyed making *Heartsounds*, which allowed her to get back to television—the medium she loved—and yet take the time to explore a character in depth and a dramatic theme with substance, as she had done in *Ordinary People*. Robert's shuttle flights to Toronto helped ease the pain of their first separation, and they even managed to squeeze in a side trip to Niagara Falls one weekend.

Still, it was more than seven years since *The Mary Tyler Moore Show* had folded and Mary was anxious to get back to her original métier. "I'd much rather do comedy next," she told reporters on her last day of shooting *Heartsounds*, "maybe three in a row. I'd love to make people laugh again."

Indeed, the time might be ripe for Mary's return to the situation-comedy scene. Suddenly, after a long dry spell, comedy shows with intelligence were starting to make a dent in the ratings—and those shows particularly abounded with interesting roles for women. The trend began with NBC's *Cheers* in the fall of 1982, which pitted a brainy, sophisticated (albeit neurotic) Shelley Long against a brawny, chauvinistic, womanizing Ted Danson (Shelley won an Emmy for her comic portrayal of brainy barmaid Diane Chambers). Pretty soon there was *Kate & Allie* (Susan Saint James and Jane Curtin), not to mention Judith

Light as a high-powered career woman and single mom in *Who's the Boss?*, Mary McDonnell as a chief of emergency medicine (and the bane of Elliott Gould's life) in *E/R*, and Susan Clark as a successful businesswoman and home-maker on *Webster*. Even TV's perennial mother-knows-best roles were moving out of the kitchen and into the white-collar professional sphere as the fall of 1984 season kicked off. On *The Cosby Show*, Bill Cosby and his TV wife, Phylicia Ayers-Allen, play the parents of five kids; but along with PTA obligations and car pools, Mom also manages to be a very successful attorney. On *Charles in Charge*, the situation is pretty much the same. Jill Pembroke (Julie Cobb), mother of three, writes restaurant reviews for the local newspaper, while houseboy Scott Baio minds the kids and mends the laundry.

Ironically, while Mary was looking around for a possible niche for herself in sitcomland again, NBC was introducing a brand-new show, *Sara*, which the network publicized as "The *Mary Tyler Moore Show* of the '80s." Sara, played by Geena Davis (who got her TV start on Dabney Coleman's short-lived *Buffalo Bill* series), was a fledgling attorney working in a San Francisco law office, surrounded by a wacky ensemble of office characters (much like the WJM newsroom crowd). There was even a best friend more than vaguely reminiscent of Rhoda Morgenstern. In previewing Sara, *Newsweek*'s Harry F. Waters noted that Geena Davis's character "manages to almost exactly replicate MTM's en-dearing blend of ingenuous effervescence and droll insouciance." He neglected to mention, though, that Geena's Davis's presence on screen as a kind of MTM reincarnation only serves to point up the fact that the real Mary Tyler Moore is no longer the cute and thirtyish career girl we like to remember. She is now barely two years away from her fiftieth birthday.

When Mary finished *Six Weeks*, she didn't work for another two years. Instead, she took the time to renovate her Manhattan apartment from top to bottom, knocking down walls, redesigning rooms, turning it from a nondescript residence into a place that she could truly call home. But after doing *Heartsounds*, Mary didn't waste any time moving into her next project—*Finnegan, Begin Again*, a movie for Home Box Office.

In the movie, Mary was cast as a widowed high school teacher who becomes romantically involved with an aging lovelorn columnist (played by Robert Preston). The result of this attachment leads her to break off a long-running affair she's been having with a married man (Sam Waterston).

Finnegan, Begin Again was written by novice screenwriter Walter Lockwood and was originally purchased by MTM Enterprises as a movie vehicle for Mary, but no major Hollywood studio would agree to make it. According to Mary, the script had some "rough edges" that needed ironing out. It may also be that—considering the youth movement in films today—the idea of a love story between a forty-five-year-old woman and a sixty-five-year-old man didn't seem like a good financial risk. At that point, cable TV came to the rescue. Home Box Office bought the script from MTM (with Mary as the star) and brought in Gower Frost, an English producer, to take over the production reins. Frost was able to get Zenith Films, an English company, to co-finance the movie.

Finnegan, Begin Again was filmed on location in Richmond, Virginia, for six weeks during the summer of 1984. Once again Mary and her leading man discovered they had some friends in common. Preston had been featured in *Victor/Victoria*, a film that co-starred James Garner and Julie Andrews. By the time production got under way,

Mary thought all the kinks in the script had been ironed out, but at first rehearsal it was obvious that the screenplay still needed work. Mary decided to approach the problem as she would have handled things on *The Mary Tyler Moore Show*. Before any film was shot, the cast held an intensive, week-long round of rehearsals, cutting, adding, and reshaping things to make the story come alive. Their improvisations were taped, so they could later watch and critique their own work and see in what new directions the script was going.

Joan Micklin Silver, the film's director, found it an exciting way to work. "We had some fabulous basic material to work with," she told Clarke Taylor of the *Los Angeles Times*. The changes, she said, were merely a matter of "thinning scenes out and letting actors who know how to make dialogue crackle find their characters."

Although Walter Lockwood's original script was difficult to classify as either a comedy or a drama—it seems to waver between both—by the time Mary, Robert Preston, and Sam Waterston had put their stamp on it, it was definitely a comedy. Mary admitted that there was still a huge dose of pathos in *Finnegan, Begin Again,* but it remained the most lighthearted piece of material she had done since leaving MTM.

Perhaps Mary had finally had her fill of heavy drama. *Ordinary People, Whose Life Is It, Anyway?, Six Weeks,* and *Heartsounds* were all therapeutic in one way or another, but now Mary had put all her ghosts behind her and she was finally done with mourning and regrets. Without question, it was Robert Levine's presence in her life that made the difference. She was drawing closer to her parents, sharing things with them in a way she had never done before. Ironically, it was her move away from them—after she left Grant Tinker and Los Angeles—that made Mary aware of how much she really needed them. Not having them just a car ride away suddenly made her want to call and visit more often. In the summer of 1983, when she and Robert rented a beach house at Quogue, Mary's folks spent two weeks with them. "It was so much fun just to be a family," Mary said, with everyone sitting around reading, doing crossword puzzles, playing cards, or just lying in the sun and watching the ocean.

At one point in her life, Mary had felt it was very important to play an independent woman—and she fought hard not to let Mary Richards be dependent on anyone when *The Mary Tyler Moore Show* was first being fashioned for the airwaves. Perhaps that's because at that point in her own life Mary had never really experienced true independence, and she wanted to live vicariously through her TV character. But in recent years Mary has mellowed. After her divorce from Grant Tinker, she spent nearly four years alone in New York before giving up the single life to marry Robert Levine. She had not only had her taste of independence—she had actually learned to adjust to it—when Robert came along. Mary jokes that just when she had finally remodeled her apartment to fit her needs as a self-sufficient single woman, Robert came into her life. It does seem that fate enjoys playing mischievous tricks on us.

Just as Mary no longer finds independence the be-all and end-all of her existence, she's no longer afraid to admit to imperfection. In September 1984 she was admitted to the Betty Ford Center in Rancho Mirage, California, for treatment of alcohol-related problems which were adversely affecting her diabetes. While most Hollywood observers gave Mary credit for the determination and courage it took to go public with her problem, the admission nevertheless stunned her fans. Dependency problems were the kind of out-of-control behavior patterns we associated with flam-

boyant and unstable personalities like Judy Garland and
Marilyn Monroe, not with someone as down-to-earth and
responsible as Mary.

Of course, Mary had been through an incredible ordeal
—several of them, in fact—during the last few years: divorce, the death of her sister and her son, career slides and
comebacks, and a total change in lifestyle as she moved
from one coast back to the other. The last two years had
been particularly wearing on her. Both of Mary's parents
had been ill: her mother had suffered a stroke in 1982; her
father had a serious abdominal problem. At the same time
that she was trying to build a new life for herself with
Robert Levine, she was suddenly making movies again in
rapid succession (*Heartsounds; Finnegan, Begin Again*). The
total sum of all those elements of upheaval had been a
terrible strain on her.

Still, the Betty Ford clinic seemed a little severe. Or was
it? The Betty Ford Center was founded in 1982 by the former First Lady and two other recovered alcoholics, and
since then more than a thousand patients have flocked there
to benefit from the center's unique program for treatment
of drug and alcohol dependency. Elizabeth Taylor was the
first show-business luminary to voluntarily enter the clinic,
and since her publicized recovery many other stars have
followed suit. Robert Mitchum was treated for alcoholism
there, Liza Minnelli and Tony Curtis became patients for
the same reason. Eileen Brennan sought out the clinic to
help her overcome an addiction to painkilling drugs in the
wake of a debilitating car accident.

The program at the Betty Ford Center is a combination
of "tough love" and psychological counseling. Patients
must be able to function without drugs or alcohol before
they enroll in the program. The center is not a detoxifica-
tion unit; its purpose is strictly rehabilitation.

Mary was by no means a drunk; but her need to indulge in social drinking (up to three or four cocktails a day) was undermining her body's chemistry. For a diabetic, that can ultimately be fatal. When Mary started having attacks of weakness and blurry vision, her husband became concerned. He realized that she was suffering from recurring spells of hypoglycemia, which meant that her blood-sugar level was dangerously low. The hypoglycemia was brought on by drinking.

By the time Mary finished working on *Heartsounds* and *Finnegan, Begin Again* in rapid succession, her episodes of weakness were becoming more and more frequent. Levine charted her blood chemistry for two weeks and noticed that when Mary eliminated her after-dinner cocktail, her blood picture improved. He worried that, unless positive measures were taken, Mary's diabetes might deteriorate and lead to such complications as blindness or kidney failure. After consultation with Mary's physicians, both she and Robert agreed that the Betty Ford Center might be the perfect place for her to get a handle on the whole thing.

In September, Mary checked into the center. Like all patients who come there, she had to sign a statement pledging that she would take an active part in the therapy program, try to be a cooperative patient, and abstain from using alcohol, drugs, or other chemicals. During her first week there, she was allowed no phone calls and no contact with her family. She was also given chores to do and had to endure daily therapy meetings, where patients were encouraged to be brutally honest with each other. For Mary, who has spent an entire lifetime building walls to keep people out, that was the toughest part of the program. But she came through like a trouper and upon "graduating" was given a medallion symbolizing her commitment to recovery.

When Mary left Rancho Mirage, she reportedly was "looking like a million" and feeling better than ever. A spokesman for the clinic said, "Her problem was not as bad as most of the patients' since she was not a heavy drinker, just a social drinker, which had a bad effect on her because she is under medication for diabetes."

Less than a week after her release from the rehabilitation center, Robert and Mary went bicycling together in New York's Central Park. According to the *Daily News*, "the couple looked just like two other ordinary people and hardly got a second glance from other Sunday weekenders in the park." Mary was obviously back in running form, because when she and Robert returned to their apartment building—and spied a photographer waiting at the entrance—they made a mad dash through an alleyway and entered the building through a service entrance.

Mary was hoping to get right back to work with *Something in Common*, an Orion picture directed by Mary's old colleague Allan Burns of the *MTM* show. But as 1984 ended, production was stymied by a number of delays. Script revisions were needed. Then Susan Sarandon, who was slated to be Mary's co-star, had to drop out of the project due to pregnancy. Early in 1985 a top Orion executive announced, "We're waiting for them to finish casting and put all the other pieces together. Right now I have no idea when the picture will shoot."

But, whatever the outcome of *Something in Common*, Mary had no intention of just standing still. By the spring of 1985 she was finally ready to do the one thing her fans had been hoping for all along—return to network television on a weekly basis. On June 24, 1985, CBS announced that they had reached a major agreement with Mary Tyler Moore. She would star in a new, half-hour situation-comedy series for them; and the show, tentatively called *Mary*, would begin production in Los Angeles in September 1985. It would probably air as a midseason replacement early in 1986.

The storyline called for Mary to play a divorced journalist who leaves a high-fashion glamour magazine to work for one of Chicago's smaller daily newspapers. In her new job, she gets assigned to write a "Helpline" column. It winds up involving her in all kinds of problems which her readers bring to her attention and her acting as an angel of mercy on their behalf. She also finds herself at constant loggerheads with her newsroom boss, but unwillingly attracted to him at the same time.

For Mary, the role seemed tailor-made. She'd been itching to play a divorcée ever since she first tried (unsuccessfully) to sell the idea to CBS in 1970. Portraying a journalist also appealed to her ever since she'd played Betty Rollin in *First, You Cry* and Martha Lear in *Heartsounds*—two real-life newswomen.

Most of all, Mary would be doing comedy again—and that's what really delighted her. The fact that *The Cosby Show* had finished number three in the Nielsens (for the 1984–85 TV season) and that shows like *Cheers, Kate & Allie,* and *Newhart* had all turned into top-20 hits gave her high hopes that intelligent comedy was back in style with a bang —and that her show would succeed, too. Her new production/writing team—David Isaacs and Ken Levine—were also the cream of the crop. In the past, they'd served as executive script consultants for *M*A*S*H* and *Cheers.*

If *Mary* takes off, Mrs. Robert Levine could be adding more Emmies to her huge stockpile of gold statuettes (and the couple might have to sell their New York co-op and relocate in Hollywood). Even if that doesn't turn out to be the case, it's obvious that Mary Tyler Moore plans to stay in the limelight. "I could never retire," she once said. "Not working would be like not breathing. Work is too much a part of me. I don't sit well. I'm a worrier but I'm also an optimist."

Whatever the future holds, she's already succeeded far beyond the wildest dreams of that little Hotpoint Pixie who danced on stoves and refrigerators. First, Mary made an enormous contribution to the development of situation comedy, then she left both Laura Petrie and Mary Richards far behind as she broke new ground. In the last decade, she has proven herself as a dramatic actress in films and theater. She has moved audiences immensely—touching their hearts and lifting their spirits in a wide range of roles, from the devoted wife of *Heartsounds* to the alienated mother of *Ordinary People* to the courageous quadriplegic of *Whose Life Is It, Anyway?* Now, as she nears the half-century mark of her life, what lies ahead for her?

Aside from the success or failure of her new TV series, there are many exciting projects that could still await her.

February 1987—the same year that Mary turns fifty—will mark the tenth anniversary of the demise of *The Mary Tyler Moore Show,* and there's always the possibility of rounding up the whole gang—Mary, Valerie Harper, Ed Asner, Ted Knight, Gavin MacLeod, Cloris Leachman, Betty White, and Georgia Engel—for a gala reunion special on CBS.

Who knows? At some point Mary might even make one other dream come true and try her luck with a Broadway musical again. Maybe not originate a part, but star in a lavish revival of a 1960s hit. A surefire show like *Mame* or *A Little Night Music* would be perfect for her.

Whatever the future holds for her, Mary Tyler Moore will always have a special place in our hearts and minds. She is a symbol of the innocence of the 1960s, tempered by the wisdom of the '80s—and she has lived her life guided by a strong inner light that brings out the best in nearly everyone she touches. She has, it seems, a spirit that can't be broken, a sense of honor that never falters, and a quiet courage that must be admired.

Grant Tinker, Dick Van Dyke, Carl Reiner, Ed Asner, Valerie Harper, Robert Redford, James Garner, and so many others would surely agree that their lives have all been enriched for having known and laughed with and loved a woman named Mary Tyler Moore.

Robert Redford once thought of her as "the all-American girl." That time is past, but Mary is now perhaps "the all-American woman." Through her work and her personal life, she has shown that independence and accomplishment are what femininity is all about.

Index